SANTIAGO CALATRAVA

ALEXANDER TZONIS

SANTIAGO CALATRAVA

THE ATHENS OLYMPICS

RIZZOLI
NEW YORK

First published in the United States of America in 2005 by
Rizzoli International Publications, Inc.
300 Park Avenue South
New York, NY 10010
www.rizzoliusa.com

2005 2006 2007 2008 / 10 9 8 7 6 5 4 3 2 1

ISBN: 0-8478-2789-5
Library of Congress Control Number: 2005928918

Designed by HvAD
Henk van Assen and Amanda Bowers

Printed in the United States of America

CONTENTS

ACKNOWLEDGMENTS

This book represents a merging of three different themes: the world of the Olympic Games, Calatrava's studies for athletic facilities, and Calatrava's sketches of the human body in movement. Each could have been a book in itself. What brought these themes into this compact synthesis are a fascinating work, a unique occasion, and a singular place: Calatrava's structures for the 2004 Olympic Games in Athens.

I wish to acknowledge my debt to friends and colleagues who helped in many ways in the making of this book: Leonidas Kikiras; Michael Krumme of the Deutsches Archäologisches Institut of Athens; Alan Karchmer; Michael Levin; Fritz Schroeder; Dimitri Balamotis; Liane Lefaivre; and Stathis Eustathiadis. My thanks to Santiago and Tina Calatrava who have generously offered their collaboration and support. My gratitude to the staff of Santiago Calatrava, S.A.; Kim Marangoni; Christof Mühlemann; all members of the Design Knowledge Systems Research Center of the Technical University of Delft; my secretary Janneke Arkesteijn; my collaborator Rebeca Caso Donadei; my publisher for special patience and trust; my editor Isabel Venero; and the staff at Rizzoli.

This book is dedicated to Sofia Calatrava in memory of her *agon*: climbing the steps of Hydra the day before the Athens games began.

OPPOSITE
**Detail of Olympic Stadium
roof in Athens**

I

AGON

The idea that the ancient Olympic Games were the result of the Greeks' obsessive competitiveness is valid only if the premodern incarnation of the games is viewed very narrowly. The Olympiads stood for more than competition: the Greek term for athletic games, *athletikoi agones,* literally translated means "prize-winning assembly." The root of the first word, *athlon,* means "contest prize," a reward bestowed on a person for some sort of achievement. The root of the second word, *agon,* means a type of ritualistic gathering, a term that connotes community. Prize-winning assemblies were a type of celebration that was common in ancient Greece, and they played an important role in the construction of Greek life. In addition to sports, they involved contests in various disciplines of the arts, including music, drama, poetry, and sculpture. While rivalry and competition were ostensibly the bases on which the games functioned, they were not the main reasons for bringing people together. Rivalry and competition were more a means than an end, the real goal being a sense of community among the participants and a celebration of the search for what the Greeks called *teliotis.* "Excellence" and "perfection" are common translations of this ancient concept. More appropriate translations, however, are "coherence," "cohesion," and perhaps "harmony," as in the desire to bring back order and normalcy. It is the ideas of community and the celebration of harmony that are the basis of the affinity between the spirit of the Olympic Games and Santiago Calatrava's architecture.

There is a profound kinship between his work and the performance of the athletes, in which *teliotis* is achieved by overcoming the constraints of gravity, materials, and the limits of the human body by means of extraordinary feats of both physical and mental strength. They both demonstrate a poetics of movement, a phrase I have used frequently to describe Calatrava's work.

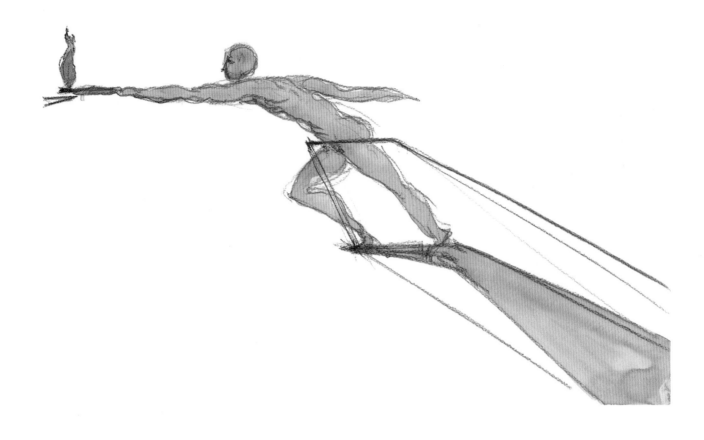

BELOW
View of Olympia with the
Kronos Hill in the background

OPPOSITE
View of Olympia with the
Alfeios River in the background

It is clear that choosing a designer whose work made manifest the ancient ideals of the Olympics was of paramount importance to the Olympic organizing committee for the 2004 games in Athens, and Calatrava emerged as the one whose work was endowed most thoughtfully and skillfully with these ideas. Before discussing these projects, it is necessary to understand a bit of the history of the Olympic Games and the architecture built to house the events of the games, both ancient and modern.

* * *

Scholars believe that the roots of Greek athletic competitions are initiation rites to adulthood and ritual funereal contests, such as those organized by Achilles to honor the memory of his fallen friend Patroklos that Homer refers to in the *Iliad*. The exact origins of the games in Olympia, however, are not known, and this is partly due to being intertwined with the myths of the era. Some traditions claimed that the hero Pelops instituted the games

to commemorate the death of Oinomaos during a chariot race. Pindar, the great poet of ancient Greece, asserts in one of his "Olympian Odes" (Ol. 10.46–47) that Heracles founded them to celebrate one of his achievements, but also to promote unity and perform a rite of purification to atone for an act of violence he had committed.

According to the "Ode," Heracles brought together the crowd and his spoils and created a sanctuary where he offered sacrifices. He then declared that a festival would be celebrated every four years. Whether the games originated with Pelops or with Heracles, it is evident that they were founded to make amends for violent acts that disrupted orderly daily life.

The sanctuary of Olympia is situated along the banks of the Alfeios River. It had provided passage to the northwest Peloponnese at the point where it joined the Cladeus River, next to the Hill of Kronos (the father of the gods). The site was fertile and rich in vegetation. Greeks believed that the wild olives that grew amply there were brought from the land of the Hyperboreans and planted by Heracles himself. The victory crowns (an object associated with funeral rites) given to athletes participating in the games were made from

branches cut from an olive tree growing behind the Temple of Zeus. Scholars have argued that the fecundity of the area considerably helped in raising enough animals for the sacrifices and well-attended feasts, allowing the games to quickly grow in popularity and ensuring their success. A sacred grove and a cult of Zeus,

Hera, and other gods existed on the site from the tenth century BCE, possibly before the institution of the games. The site's importance during this period is attested to by the remains of sacrifices, the great ash altar of Zeus, altars to Earth (Gaia), Themis, and Hera, among other deities, as well as votive offerings, figurines, metal objects, tripods, and cauldrons with three legs that were probably dedicated by Peloponnesian chiefs who used the area for rituals and meetings.

The first written document explicitly related to the games is a list of Olympic victors (in fact, it is the second oldest document of Greek writing) and is dated 776 BCE. From 776 until 724, the only competition that happened during the festival was the *stadion,* a race that took its name from the ancient unit of measurement (the equivalent of approximately 192 meters). The race started a *stadion* distance from the altar of Zeus, which was simply a heap of ash, in front of which stood a priest who signaled the start of the race by raising a torch. The winner would receive the torch upon finishing and set fire to the consecrated parts of the sacrificed animals placed on the altar. (When the games eventually included more than one competition, this race would mark the beginning of the games.)

The torch relay of the modern Olympics has its origins in this ritual, though it no longer retains the religious overtones. In 724 a second race was added, the *diaulos,* which was the distance of two *stadia.* The discus, javelin throw, high jump, and wrestling were introduced in 708 and boxing in 688. Horse races were introduced later: the four-horse race in 680 and horseback riding in 648. A race in which the participants wore armor was the last addition to the ancient games in 520.

OPPOSITE
The sculptures of legendary
athletes Kleobis and Biton.
Delphi Museum

At various times during these two hundred years, a game was introduced only to be dropped a few years later. It is not entirely clear why a new game was introduced. What is known is that it had to meet two criteria: that it was popular and digni-fied. Another important contributing factor to the evolution of the games was that the events were continually subject to evaluation to determine how they could best measure the performance of the athletes. New rules were developed, as were new methods for conducting the various contests.

The organizers aimed for perfection in this regard. This was not a pre-established standard but one based on experience and the consideration of many alternatives, from which emerged an informed judgment—a process the Greeks called *crisis.*

The Olympics were the most important of all the ancient festivals of games, though many other sanctuaries and city-states hosted them. In fact, the sanctuary of Olympia hosted games, which included contests related to the arts, that were similar to the Olympics before the institution was officially founded. Unlike these other games—both in Olympia and elsewhere—the Olympics did not have poetry, music, or acting contests. It did, however, have trumpet and herald competi-tions, which were very necessary to the games to mark events and make announcements. The winners were treated as honorably as the athletes, suggesting the importance of contests unrelated to sports to promote principles of excellence. Despite the absence of contests related to writing and art in the Olympics, Olympia was nevertheless an important center for writers and painters to share their work with the public. It was here that Herodotus had a public reading of his *History* from the back porch of the Temple of Zeus.

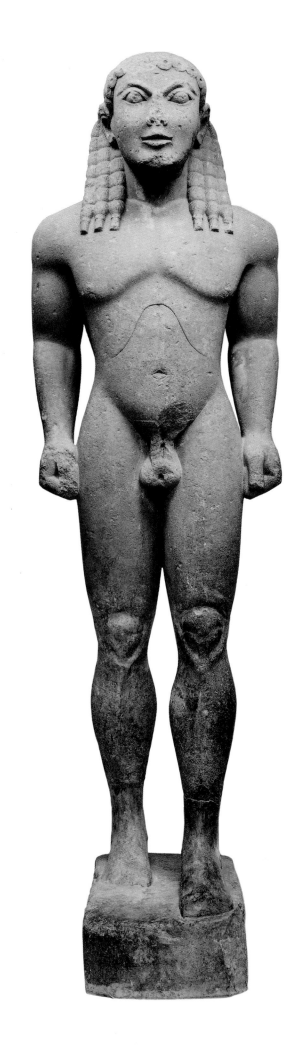

The sanctuary of Delphi also hosted games, and these are considered second in importance to those of Olympia. It was here that the renowned statues of the legendary figures Kleobis and Biton were placed in 590 BCE, the first to honor athletes. It celebrated not only their physical perfection but also their supreme sacrifice: they died while coming to the aid of their aged mother. In Delphi, unlike Olympia, the games included poetry and music competitions.

Why did various sanctuaries and city-states decide to host games, and why did the games in Olympia and Delphi develop into the most important of those competitions? Many ancient sanctuaries immediately outside urban centers were founded in locations where there were territorial disputes between city-states. One theory is that the games were held in these areas so the city could claim the land as theirs. But this was not the case with Olympia or Delphi, as neither sanctuary was located on a disputed border. On the contrary, they were situated away from contested territories

in the cross hairs of the routes formed by Greek city-states that had contact with one another. Their location guaranteed that the games were not tied to any specific city-state or center of power. As relatively neutral territories, Olympia and Delphi could attract and bring together the expanding world of diverse Greek city-states and city-colonies to enable the growth of what scholar Gregory Nagy has called "panhellenism."

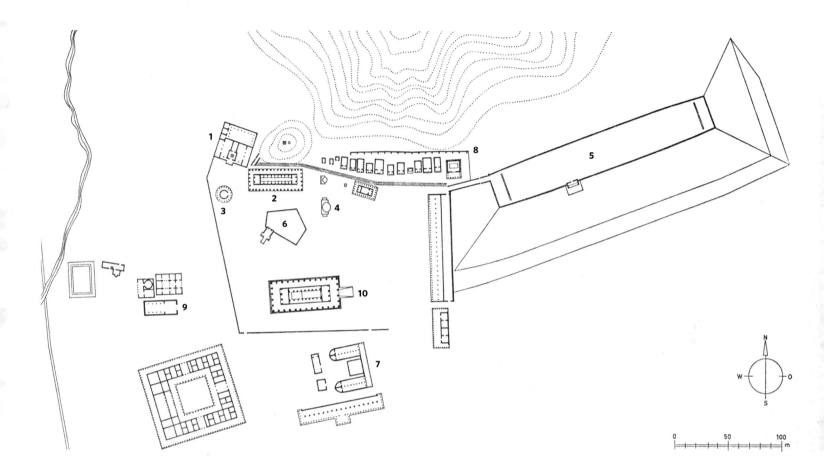

General plan of Olympia in
the archaic period (sixth
and early fifth centuries BCE).
After Herrmann, 1972

1 Prytaneion

2 Temple of Hera

3 Philippeum

4 Altar of Zeus

5 Stadium

6 Pelopion

7 Bouleuterion

8 Row of treasuries

9 Phidias's workshop

10 Temple of Zeus

The games were a place where not only athletes competed, but also the city-states they came from through their donations to the sanctuary and the erection of commemorative statues of the victors. Victory was also celebrated by poetry commissioned from professional poets. The *epinikion,* as the victory poem was called, extolled the winner, his city of origin, and the city's gods and heroes. In Olympia, the Philippeum was erected as a form of propaganda by Philip, king of Macedonia, to celebrate his triumph over the rest of the Greeks in Chaironeia. But it is also true that the games were intended to create a sense of community, as exemplified by the *diaulos,* the most important event of the games. It was organized with the express purpose to promote unity among the participants, as W. Burkert describes: "When the Eleans made their sacrifice [to Zeus], all the Greek envoys present had to sacrifice. But in order that their procession not be delayed, the runners ran one stadium length away from the altar [of Zeus] as if calling on the [Greek envoys] to come, then turned and ran back as if to announce that all of Greece was arriving to share in the joy." It seems the role of the sanctuary of Olympia and the games was largely therapeutic in resolving conflicts between city-states, fostering a sense of common identity between tribal communities, and creating a "melting pot" of the various regional cultures of the Hellenic world by inviting them to participate. This explains the overt references to conflict and violence in the founding myths of the Olympics and the role of the *agon,* the ritualistic gathering, which involved purification rites designed to restore order. The importance of this aspect of the games is further understood when one considers the inviolacy of the territory of Elis and the sanctuary of Olympia, which was rarely broken, and the sacred truce. (Elis is a traditional rural town located northwest of Olympia that controlled the sanctuary and supervised the games.) Throughout its premodern, thousand-year history, the Olympics were held in August or early September for four to six days (a period that included a full moon), during which no fighting between Greeks was permitted.

The site of Olympia was flat and squarish. It was dominated by temples and public buildings related to the games, but not by arenas or sports grounds, as is the case with contemporary Olympic sites. Scholars believe that the earliest stadium was probably a simple runway situated inside the Altis, close to the Altar of Zeus. A later stadium, which still exists today, was also a simple structure that used the incline of the hill to create seating for the spectators. By the third century BCE, the site included, in addition to temples, the Prytaneion, a dining hall some believe was for the winners; the Metroon, the Temple of the Mother of the Gods; Leonidaion, an atrium-shaped building used as a type of hotel; the *katagogion,* the Shrine of Hestia; the Stoa of Echo (later rebuilt in the fourth century); the Pelopion, the Tomb of Pelops; the Bouleuterion, a meeting place of the Council of the Games; the Temple of Zeus; the Temple of Hera; the Philippeum; and assorted altars and statues. At the Bouleuterion, athletes pledged a sacred oath at the beginning of the games that they were not going to violate the rules, which mandated that they were free Greek citizens—i.e., not slaves—and that they had not committed murder or sacrilege.

Spectators were subject to the rules concerning murder and sacrilege, but they did not have to be Greek citizens (though they had to be free). A row of treasuries was built by various cities (mostly Greek colonies that were participating in the games). They were intended to shelter precious offerings to the gods, but their ultimate purpose was to be a kind of advertisement for the superiority of the city that built them. Among these treasuries, that of Gela, built around 450, is the most notable for its innovative detailing and its bright-colored, terra-cotta slabs.

OPPOSITE

**Column with a Doric capital
from the Temple of Hera in
Olympia**

The Temple of Hera at Olympia was a peripteral building (a building whose cella is surrounded by a colonnade) and was the most important of the early Doric temples. Originally dedicated to Zeus as well as to Hera, it was built in 600–590 BCE on much older foundations. It is an important building because of its innovations: it was one of the earliest examples adopting the principle of "angle contraction" (achieved by placing the last two columns closer together) in the colonnade that characterized later canonical Doric buildings. It is also notable for its dimensioning and arrangement of the elements to create a harmonious overall composition. The most noteworthy feature was within the cella, which anticipated the column arrangement of the interior of the important Temple of Apollo at Bassae. In it, alternating columns were replaced by spur-walls projected into the cella. Pausanias visited the temple in the second century and wrote in his *Guide* about a wooden column that was still standing. This suggests that the original temple was wooden and that the stone construction was accomplished gradually by replacing the wood around the middle of the sixth century CE, which further attests to the evolution of the materials of ancient Greek temples from wood to stone.

The Temple of Zeus at Olympia was built with local limestone. It was constructed around 470 BCE with the short sides comprised of six columns and the long sides of thirteen columns. It was built by the town of Elis and designed, according to Pausanias, by Libo of Elis. The most striking features of the temple were its magnificent sculptures. The central *akroterion,* the figure on the peak of the roof, was made of gilded bronze and depicted Victory.

OPPOSITE
**Metope from the Temple of
Zeus in Olympia**

FOLLOWING PAGE [LEFT]
**Metope 4 of the Temple of Zeus
in Olympia**

FOLLOWING PAGE [RIGHT]
**West pediment from the Temple
of Zeus in Olympia**

While this work is not extant, one can get an idea of what it looked like from another statue, the Nike by Paionios of Mende (see pg. 46). It is a two-meter-high female figure with windblown drapery alighting a triangular base. The accompanying inscription reveals that the Messenians and Naupactian dedicated it to the Olympian Zeus and that the sculptor was Paionios of Mende, who had been a winner of an *akroteria* contest. This is further evidence of sculpture contests related to the various building projects in Olympia and that the sculptor did not only commemorate the victory of the athletes and of the heroes related to the Olympic Games but also, like Pindar in several of his "Odes," his own victory in an art contest.

Other parts of the temple represented different events, such as the pediments commemorating mythological events associated with conflict and cruelty. The east pediment depicted the myth of the chariot race between Pelops and Oenomaos, and the west pediment depicted the fight between the Centaurs and Lapiths. The interior metopes (the space between the triglyphs of the Doric frieze) depicted the Labors of Heracles. The lower architrave of the superimposed interior columns

supported a level over the aisles, creating galleries that could be visited by means of winding stairs. From these galleries, visitors could admire the colossal gold, ivory, and chryselephantine cult statue of Zeus filling the entire interior. It was considered one of the Seven Wonders of Antiquity. Phidias sculpted it, and he also created the statue of Athena Parthenos, another gold and ivory work in the Parthenon. By 457 BCE, construction of the temple was finished, and in 432 BCE Phidias began working on the statue. Archeologists have discovered the atelier where Phidias worked while making the statue on the site of the sanctuary.

The Philippeum was a *tholos,* or round building. Its construction began in 335 BCE by King Philip and was completed by Alexander the Great. An Ionic colonnade surrounded the building and a Corinthian, semidetached colonnade occupies the inner face of the cella wall and plays no structural role. The building had an overt political purpose as it housed the statues of the Macedonian royalty Amyntas, Philip, Alexander, Euridice, and Olympias made by Leochares.

By 435 CE, Emperor Theodosios II forbade the use of pagan religious buildings. While this did impact the games, they were already declining in popularity and importance. One of the main reasons for the existence of the games—to promote a sense of community among various Greek city-states—had ceased to be relevant. The games had succeeded in creating a collective (male) Greek identity and as

the ancient Hellenic world became more cohesive, a new challenge emerged: bringing together the heterogeneous cultures from beyond the Greek diaspora. With the religious aspect removed and the changing global, non-Greek community, the ancient Olympiads had very little to offer. It would take nearly fifteen hundred years before the value of the spirit and conceptual framework of the games would be recognized and reestablished, responding to the new needs for a global community.

* * *

Spurred by the unique circumstances brought about by modernity, Pierre de Fredy, the Baron de Coubertin of France (1863–1937), an aristocratic sportsman who excelled at rowing, founded an Olympic movement that lead to the first modern Olympiad in 1896. The International Olympic Committee was founded in Paris on June 23, 1894. De Coubertin became president of the committee in 1896 and held the post for twenty-nine years. The committee decided that the games would be held every four years following the old tradition.

However, as opposed to the ancient games that occurred only in one location, Olympia, the modern Olympic Games became peripatetic. The first games took place in Greece in the marble Panathinaiko Stadium in the heart of Athens— not in Olympia— with an audience of 70,000.

The building existed on the site as early as 329 BCE and was later improved by Herodus Attikos (from 139 to 194 CE). It was not associated with the ancient Olympic Games; it hosted the Panathenean festival honoring Athena (rather than Zeus as the Olympics did). Like the rest of the stadia of Greek antiquity, it was far from a feat of engineering: it made use of the natural topography of the area between two hillocks and required very little excavation. It is significant because of the quality

of the plan, its details, and its use of high quality marble from the mountain of Penteli (this marble was also used in the Parthenon). Ernst Ziller excavated and reconstructed the stadium from August 1869 to February 1870, and it was ready to receive the first modern Olympic Games in 1896. The structure remains one of the most admired works of architecture associated with the modern Olympics.

After Athens, the second games were hosted by Paris, and the third were hosted by St. Louis, Missouri. Los Angeles hosted the 1932 games in the middle of the Great Depression. The stadium was designed by father and son architects, John and Donald C. Parkinson, who introduced the open-ended, horseshoe design. This structure was one of the most important built for the Olympics because it was based on an ancient stadium.

While the ancient games were not interrupted by war, this was not the case with the modern games: the 1916 games were cancelled due to World War I and the 1940 and 1944 games due to World War II. The 1980 games in Moscow and the 1984 games in Los Angeles were partially boycotted. The most tragic event of the modern games, however, was the terrorist attack during the 1972 games in Munich, when eleven Israeli athletes were killed; this incident did not stop the games, and they resumed after a day's interruption.

Many Olympic organizations, including those of the United States, Great Britain, France, Sweden, Czechoslovakia, and the Netherlands asked for a boycott of the 1936 games in Berlin. The city had been awarded the games by the International Olympic Committee in 1931, before the Nazis came to power. An alternative People's Olympiad was planned in Barcelona, but was cancelled at the last minute due to the outbreak of the Spanish Civil War. The boycott did not succeed: the Berlin Games went on with nearly 4 million spectators from forty-nine countries and became a vehicle for promoting the ideology of the regime. They were

ideally suited to this purpose. All forms of media and culture were mobilized toward this end, including the most modern ones, radio and film. Architecture was also given a central role for the first time in the history of the modern Olympics. Some of the ideas were simplistic (and some would argue vulgar), such as the design of the Olympic Village, which was laid out in the form of the map of Germany with Berlin represented by the main dining hall. The design of the main

facilities, however, was noteworthy. Julius March, who also designed the archeological museum in Baghdad in 1936, was asked to design the German Stadium, or rather redesign it; it was originally built by his father, Otto March, in 1909 and modified later to house 110,000 spectators and a colossal marching ground for 500,000 people. Adolf Hitler found the initial proposals by March too modest and modern, so he proceeded to alter them significantly with the help of the young architect Albert Speer (who would later become Hitler's favorite architect). The intent was not only to enhance the building's sublime character but also give it a more classical appearance in order to create an explicit association between Nazi Germany and ancient Greece. It is one of the most memorable of all Olympic buildings.

Toward the same end, the German organizers "invented" one of the most thrilling and moving events of the modern games, the torch relay. This event was not part of the ancient festival but was related to the practice of the winner of the *stadion* race receiving a torch upon finishing. The torch relay was originally conceived by the German professor Dr. Carle Diem for the cancelled 1916 Berlin games. Hitler invited Diem to be part of the organizing team of the 1936 Games. A special ceremony was created to take place on the original site of the games in Olympia, in which a Greek girl in classical costume lit a "sacred" torch using a sun-focusing mirror. The torch was relayed from Greece to Berlin, a distance of more than 3,000 kilometers, through seven countries. In Berlin, it ignited a flame in a cauldron, an object with no symbolic significance or role in the ancient games.

Like the torch relay, another popular event of the modern games, the marathon, was not part of the original Olympiad. It was conceived for the 1896 Athens games by Michel Bréal, a French a philologist at the Sorbonne. It was inspired by the legend of Pheidippides, a warrior who allegedly carried the news of the Greek victory at the Battle of Marathon in September 490 BCE by running from Marathon

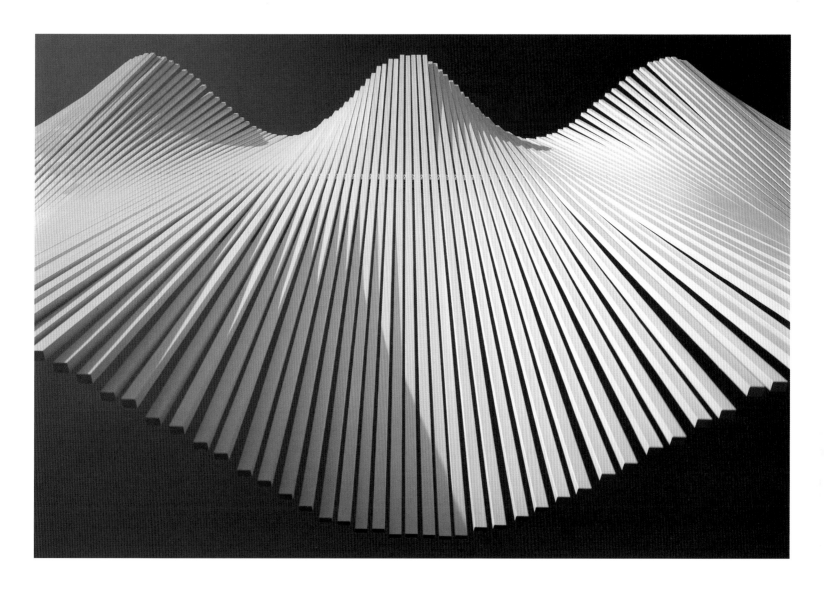

to Athens, a 40,000-meter, or 26-mile, distance. (The official distance of the marathon for the modern Olympics was later established as the distance between Windsor Castle and London Olympic Stadium during the 1948 London Olympics.) The first marathon was won by Spiridon Louis, a water carrier who was born in Marousi, a village neighboring Athens. On April 10, 1896, "wearing shoes that had been donated by his fellow villagers," he was the first runner to enter the marble Panathinaiko Stadium, creating the first record. In the 1936 Berlin Summer Olympics, Louis was a special guest of honor and was received by Hitler who offered him an olive branch from Olympia.

***

In the pantheon of great Olympic architecture, March's stadium stands alongside Calatrava's landmark work for the Athens Olympics, but for radically different reasons. Throughout the development of the project, Calatrava made calculated decisions regarding the incorporation or reinterpretation of the ideas and symbols traditionally associated with the games. He jettisoned the cauldron, which previously had been lit by a relayed torch as part of the opening ceremonies,

and replaced it with a gigantic moving torch. He created doves in the broken-tile mosaic "skin" that covers the facades of the auxiliary buildings to reference, metaphorically, the pact that mandated that no fighting among the Greeks would take place during the games.

ABOVE AND OPPOSITE
Details of Nations Wall from the Athens Olympic Sports Complex

March's stadium was static, rigorous to the point of being severe, sublime, and patently populist, all in an effort to foment fear and awe. Calatrava's dynamic structures, however, defy gravity with features that soar into the bright Athens sky. Many of them were designed to look as if they were on the brink of either falling or rising. In this way, they are closer in spirit to the Nike by Paionios of Mende discussed above, a work seemingly suspended in the "pregnant moment," which appeared ready to take off and to land simultaneously. Movement, both actual and implied, in Calatrava's structures—much like the Nike, the pediment sculpture of the Temple of Zeus, the organically inspired elements of classical buildings, and the ancient Olympic Games—is meant to inspire and restore the creative potential in those who witness it.

ABOVE
**Detail of the wall mosaic
depicting a dove from one of
the Athens Olympic Sports
Complex buildings**

OPPOSITE
Detail of Nations Wall

**Details of the Nike by Paionios
of Mende of Olympia**

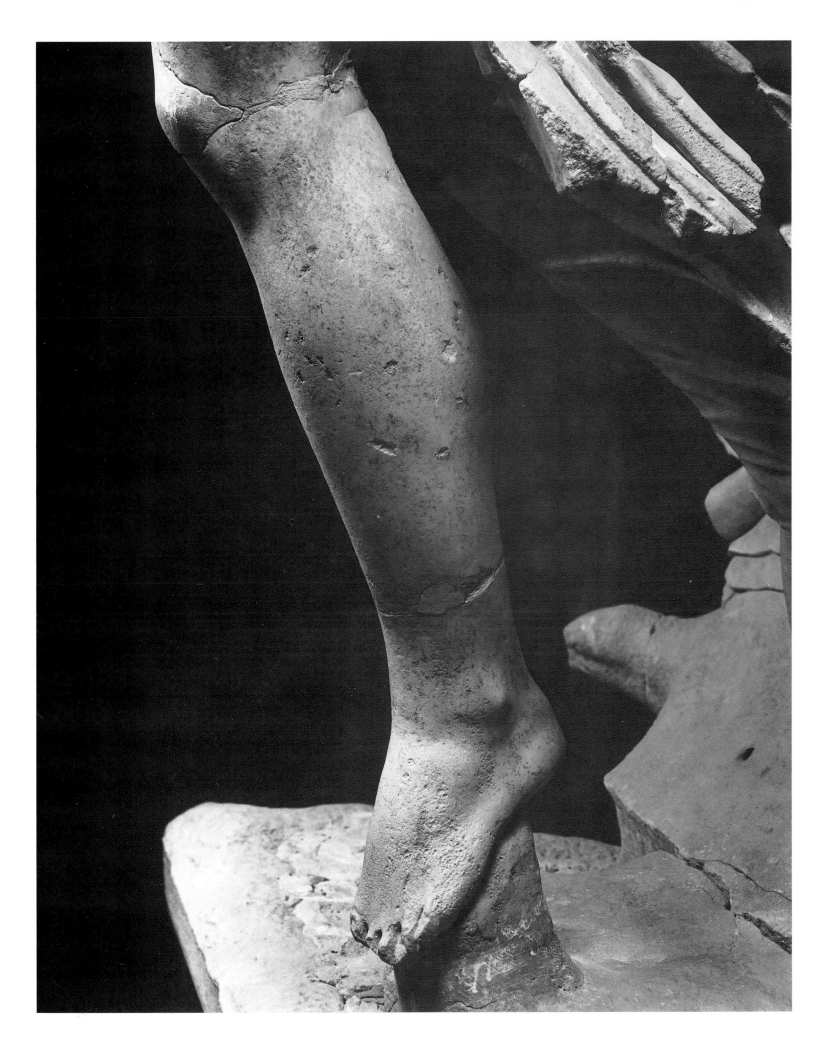

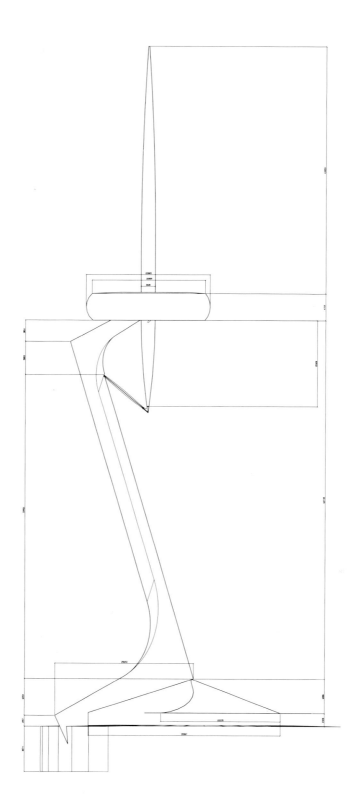

OPPOSITE
**Details of the Nike by Paionios
of Mende**

RIGHT
**Side view of Montjuic
Telecommunications Tower**

II

THE PROJECTS

Several structures in Calatrava's oeuvre are precedents for his projects for the 2004 Olympics. In fact, one of his first projects—designed a few years prior to the completion of his dissertation in 1981 at the Swiss Federal Institute of Technology (ETH) in Zurich and the establishment of his practice as an architect and engineer in the same city—was an athletic facility. The project, the roof for the IBA Squash Hall in Berlin, was for a building designed by the Swiss architects Fabio Reinhart and Bruno Reichlin. Submitted as a competition entry that was not selected ultimately, only a rough model of the work was made. What is important about this scheme by Calatrava, in relation to his future work, is that the roof structure was designed to move.

Movement in structures was the subject of his doctoral dissertation entitled *On the Foldability of Space Frames.* The aim of his research was the development of a system to enable the design of complex frame structures to create building elements—such as roofs, walls, and doors—that could be opened, closed, and formed into various shapes through a mechanical device. During the last stages of his dissertation, he created a model of a roof structure for the IBA Squash Hall using this system. The movement of the structure was simple: the sloping sides of the roof and the poles that supported them could be moved in a wavelike motion. With this, an object that seemed more like a toy than a model articulating his complex ideas, Calatrava revealed for the first time his manifesto for a poetics of movement in architecture.

Calatrava devised a structure composed of bars connected by mechanical joints that could pivot, open, lie flat, form a dome, close, and collapse by retracting into a compact rod, much like an umbrella. He discovered that as the bars with joints—referred to as linkages—moved, the frame structure functioned similar to the "legs" of a drawing compass and could trace, therefore, intricate curves, cycloids, epicycloids, cardioids, parabolas, hyperbolas, or hyperbolic paraboloids, the shape favored by Antoni Gaudí.

Model of IBA Squash Hall roof

Reminiscent of Leonardo da Vinci's drawings of flying machines and birds, the linkage-like structure of the IBA Squash Hall was a system of vertical and horizontal compression and tension members connected by joints and strings. It was a clear demonstration of his creation of folding frames for a roof, and it presented the possibility of creating a movable wall surface. In its ability to trace shapes, it also revealed its usefulness as a design tool. By observing the edges of the flapping "wings" and the leaning poles of structure, one could see a variety of curved surfaces emerging.

Through his research Calatrava devoted many critical years of his life studying the genesis of form, and he grew to be an expert not only on folding structures but also complex curved surfaces. This expertise became evident in his notable Montjuic Telecommunications Tower (1989–92) for Telefonica in Barcelona, Spain. Strictly speaking, the project is not a sports facility. It was, however, part of a major athletic event. It was linked with the 1992 Olympic Games in Barcelona. Resembling the figure of an athlete holding a torch, it became a symbol of the games and had a galvanizing effect on an otherwise dispersed Olympic complex, becoming a memorable image associated not only with the games but also with the city. Situated on the slopes of the Montjuic hill, the steel tower,

136 meters high, stands immediately next to the Palau Sant Jordi Arena designed by Arata Isozaki and overlooks the sports facilities on the site of the games. Leaning gently from a three-point foundation to coincide with the angle of the sun at the solstice, the tower's feet rest on a brick drum (a requirement of the competition). Its heel is supported by a circular shell of white concrete and is covered with broken tiles. The tower structure repeats the fundamental geometry of the base to support an annular segment, which houses an array of antennas.

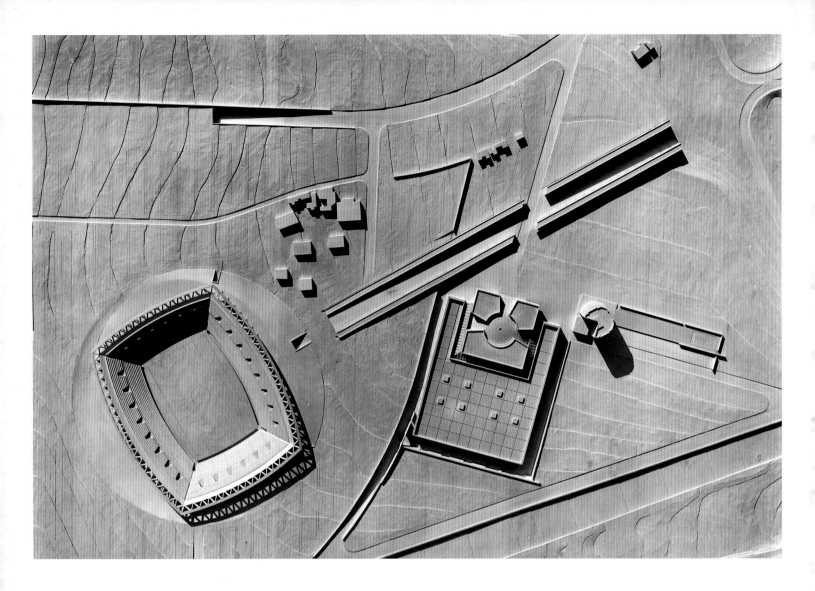

The first athletic facility designed by Calatrava was the Calabria Football Stadium (1991). The stadium was to be located 3 kilometers from the city center of Reggio Calabria, Italy with a view of Sicily across the Strait of Messina. A competition entry, in collaboration with Pier Luigi Nicolin, the scheme was conceived with the constraints of the landscape in mind and can only be approached from a central axis. The tiers are formed by a system of modular, precast-concrete interlocking units. The structure is supported by steel spindles at the rear. The roof is composed of slender, splayed beams that cantilever out from the rear of the tiers and are tied at their tips.

A year after the Calabria competition, Calatrava submitted a design for a larger athletic facility to an invitational competition for the senate of Berlin: the Jahn Olympic Sports Complex (1992). The project was part of the city's bid to host the 2000 Olympic Games and included several new sports structures. The brief requested designs for an Olympic boxing hall, a judo hall, and a district park.

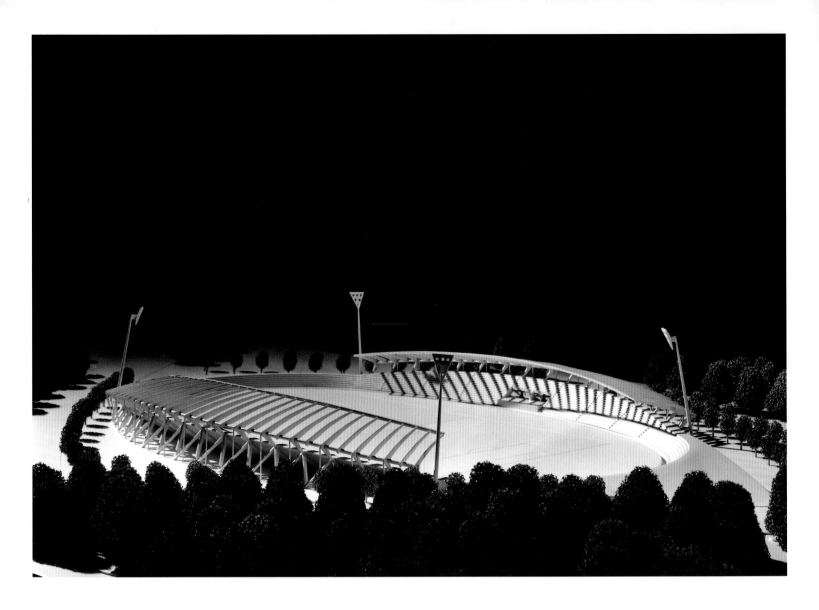

The project also included the development of a housing scheme along the old border on the western edge of Mauerpark and urban improvements, such as the layout of Falkplatz and an entrance at Bernauer and Eberswalder Strasse. The site included a border strip—created after the demolition of the Berlin Wall—that linked it to Mauerpark.

Calatrava's main preoccupation was to preserve the memory of the old city structure by giving definition to an amorphous area. To do this, he created a park with formal elements, such as the arrangement of trees, to bring together heterogeneous parts of the site and overcome the fragmentation that was inherited from history.

The two new structures designed by Calatrava are situated along the southern edge of the site to preserve the open spaces. The smaller judo hall is located across the end of the existing sports stadium, which was modified and visually integrated into the new project through various additions,

including new accesses and a roof to cover the stands. The playing fields and tennis courts were placed according to the overall geometry of the plan. Splayed concrete buttresses are used for both structures. The ends of the supporting buttresses are truncated in the smaller pavilions. The transverse roof trusses of these pavilions are suspended asymmetrically from vertical tension members attached to the steel center sections of the main arches with a lightweight, triangulated longitudinal truss.

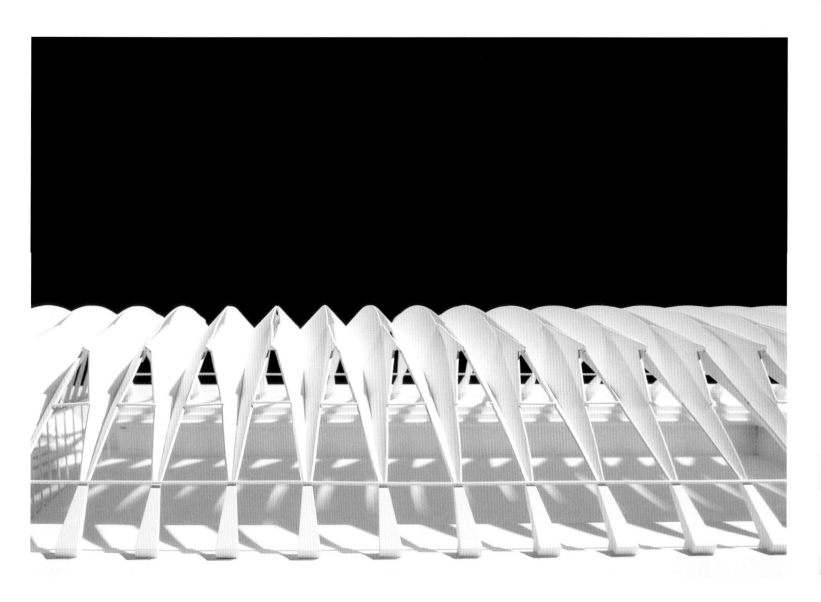

OPPOSITE
Salou Football Stadium

ABOVE
Pre Babel Sports Center, Geneva

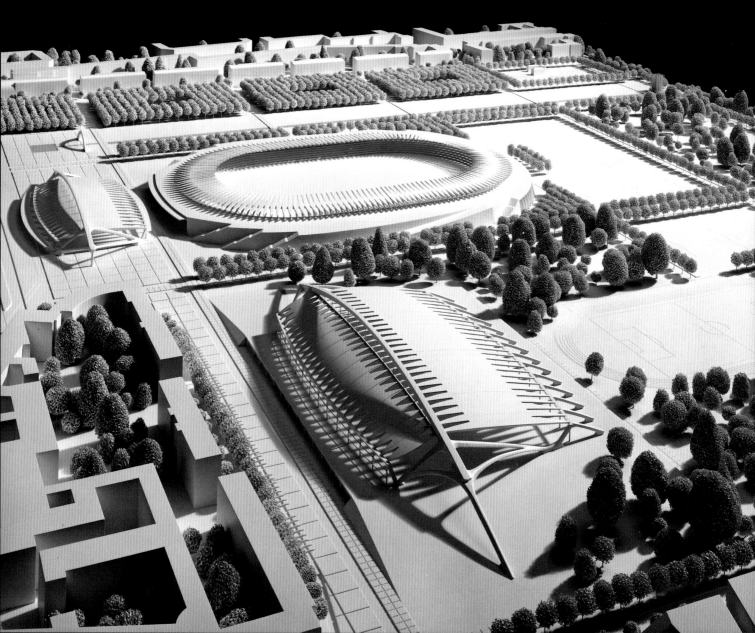

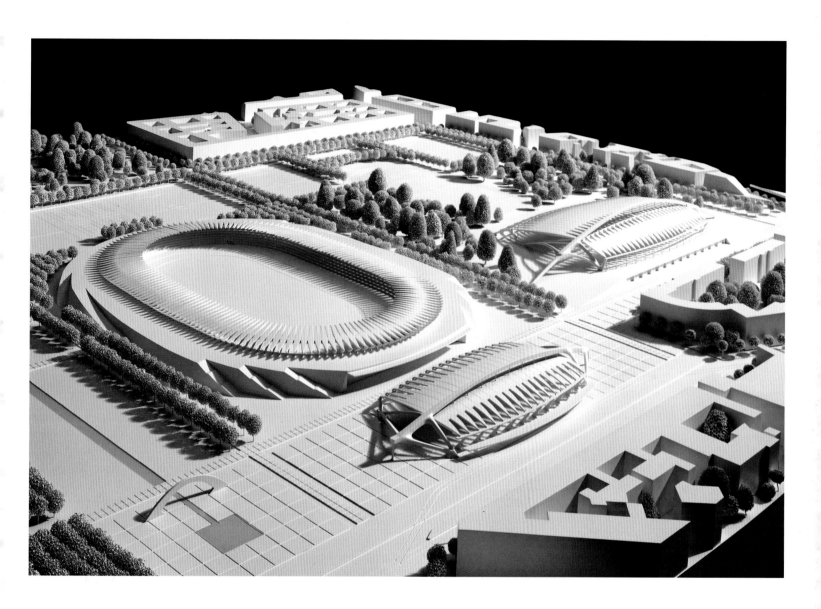

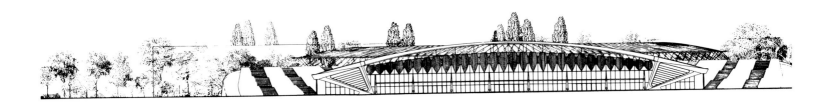

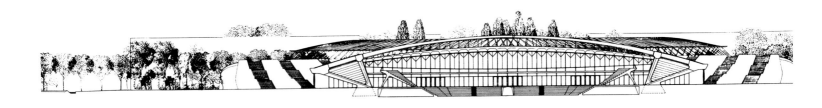

Jahn Olympic Sports Complex,
sections

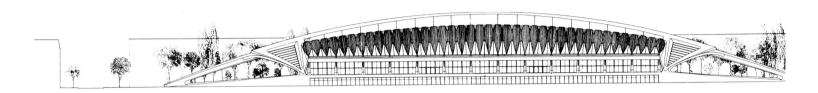

Jahn Olympic Sports Complex,
views

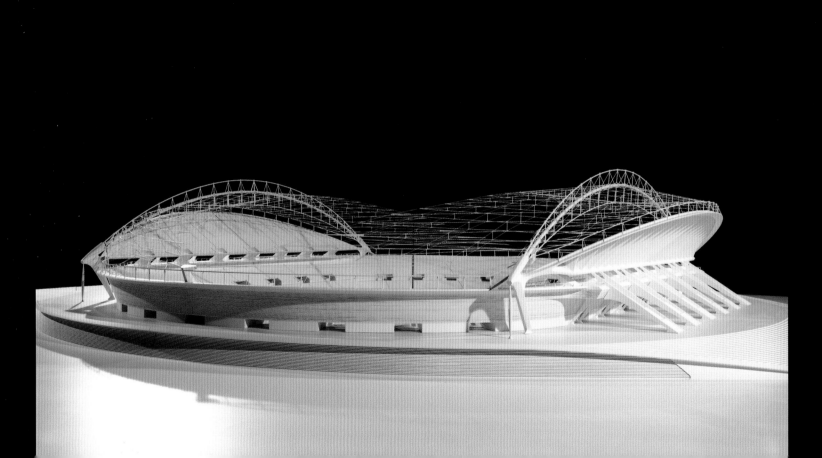

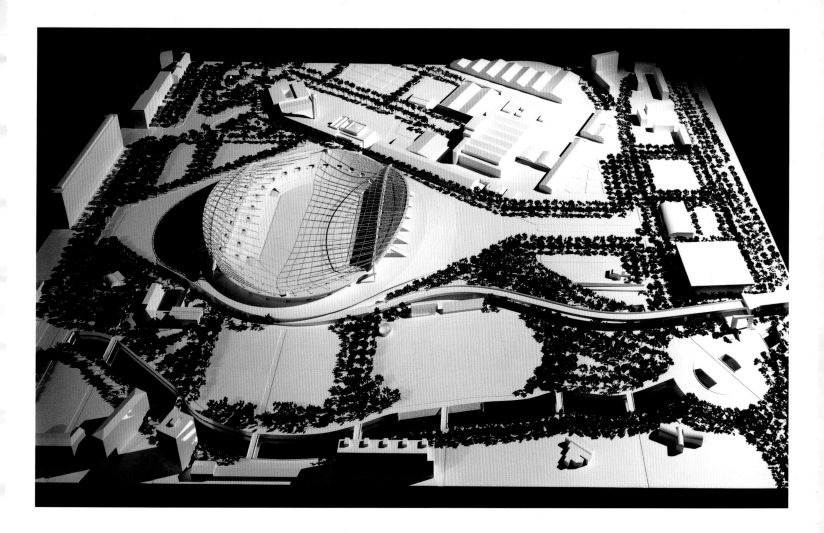

The World Cup Stadium (1995) in Marseille was an entry for a competition initiated by the city. The program asked for the reconstruction and expansion of the existing Velodrome so that it could be used as a stadium for the 1998 World Cup.

The historic Velodrome, located in the heart of a large sports park bordering the Boulevard Michelet, formed the basis of the scheme. The facility was equipped with straight-edged seating for 40,000. Calatrava's design proposed a modification of the seating and partial reconstruction to create the lower tiers. The massive addition provides extra seating in the form of new, upper tiers along the sides. A tensile roof structure provides cover for 60,000 spectators. According to the brief:

. . . two offset structural arches are balanced upon a raised, free-standing, common point of rotation at each side of the stadium. The concrete arches are stiffened by tapering ribs and are pitched to conform to the incline of the new tiers. These arches also create the required resistance to tension loads generated by a series of catenary cables hanging through and stressing the roof structure. The rod-and-cable structure of the roof is supported by a vertical, bowed steel tube with triangulated bracing, and is stabilized by the inherent tension of the system. The main stairs form the rear members of A-frames that support the access platforms. Extensions to these stairways also assist in stabilizing the new, upper-tier structure. The platforms provide direct access to the media, reception, administrative, and club spaces. Ticket areas, changing rooms and other technical spaces are housed beneath the plinths, which rise gently on the approach to each side to flank the stadium's body.

Two drawings of Velodrome
Football Stadium

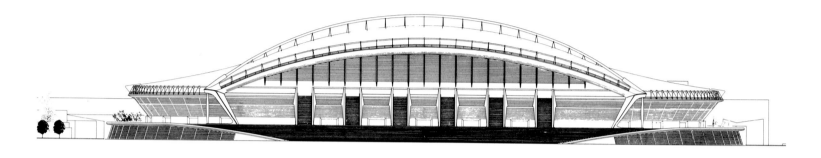

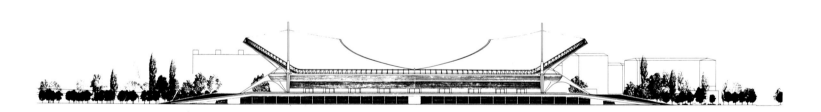

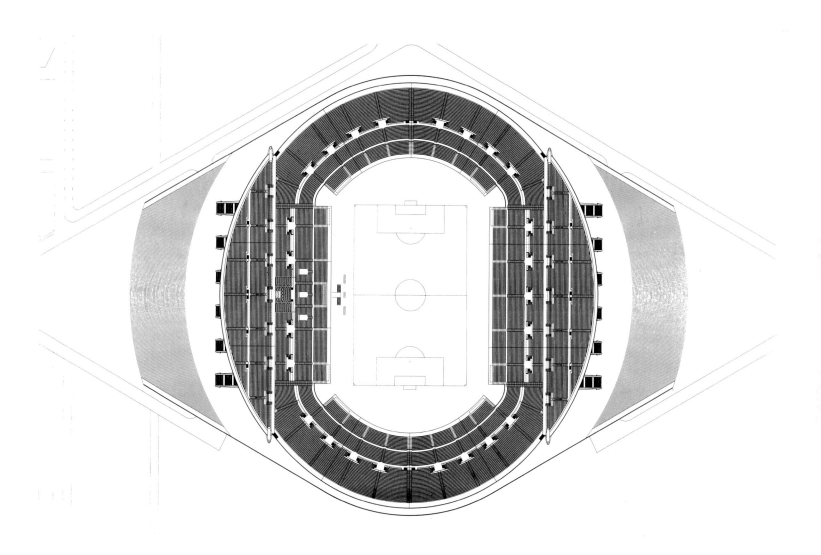

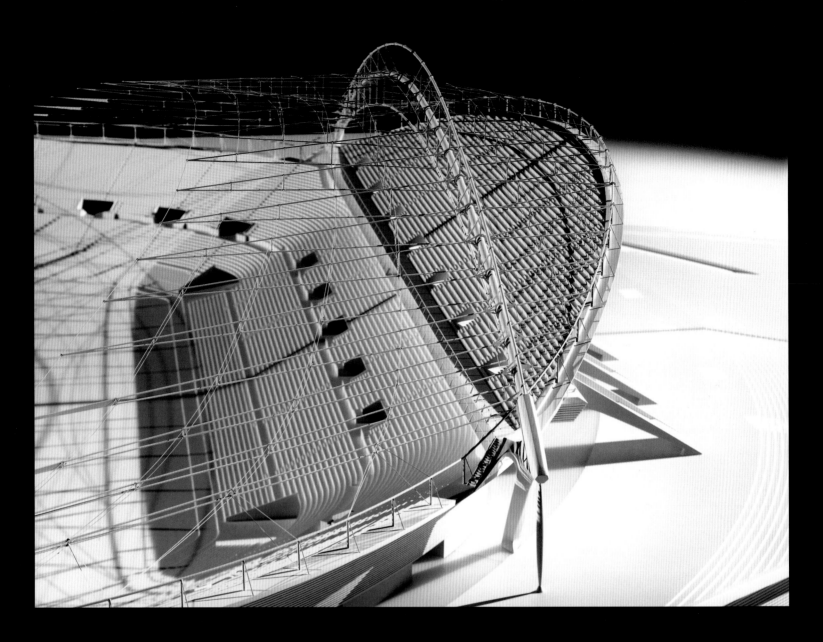

For the surrounding area, the project created two piazzas to the north and south. Access for pedestrians and vehicles was separated completely. Planting was provided for the open public areas, a feature employed in most of Calatrava's athletic projects.

A similar approach to the design of the circulation areas and the public spaces in between these areas, which needed as much attention as the buildings themselves, is evident in the schemes for the Bilbao Football Stadium (1995), the University of Maastricht (2000), and the Stadium Zurich (2000).

Stockholm made a bid for the 2004 Olympic Games. In 1996 the city government had an invitational competition for two new stadiums: the New Olympic Stadium and a smaller, warm-up facility nearby. The site, located southeast of the city on a popular ski slope, was selected after preliminary studies examined other possible locations and determined the necessary infrastructure for a new stadium. The brief asked for the main open stadium to seat 70,000, but it had to meet local demands after the games, so the capacity of the stadium had to be reduced down to 30,000. It also needed to be covered by a full roof.

The site was an artificial hill near an old industrial area that had been converted into housing. To avoid the excavation of hazardous landfill and expensive stabilization operations to preserve the hill, Calatrava proposed moving the site to the foot of the hill. Concerned with the spatial organization of the area, Calatrava felt that by placing the stadium in this location—if it was integrated into the edge of the new housing development—the stadium would create a new feature on the Hammerby Waterfront: a gateway between this new residential district and the forested Knack Park on the southeast slope of the hill. In addition, the new location would permit use of the urban transport systems under development for the waterfront, which included a tram connection, a light rail connection, a public boat service, and the southern link of the new Stockholm ring road.

The Olympic Stadium is placed parallel to the foot of the hill and serves as an acoustic barrier from the noise generated by the new ring road. Its main entrance is approached from a plaza on the nearby canal. Its secondary entrance is located to the south, and it is approached through the woods from the subway station on the other side of the artificial hill and across a wide, terraced bridge over the ring road.

The stadium had to accommodate the needs related to its long-term use, and Calatrava addressed this by means of an ingenious solution. According to the brief of the project:

... along each side, aligned with the longitudinal axis, cable-braced, curving cantilevers hung on central tubular arches forming two spherical segments covered by stretched fabric. During the Olympics, these roof canopies—anchored to pivot-points in the elevated plinth—would shade the open stands and define the silhouette of the structure.

After the Olympics,

... a cable and winch system [sic] would rotate the dynamic segments toward each other about their pivotal axes. An area of central roof glazing would then be added, and the platforms of the elevated stands would be pivoted upward to form vertical walls, thus closing the sides to create an indoor arena.

The span of the roof arches was 285 meters, and their maximum height was 70 meters above the field when open and 35 meters when closed.

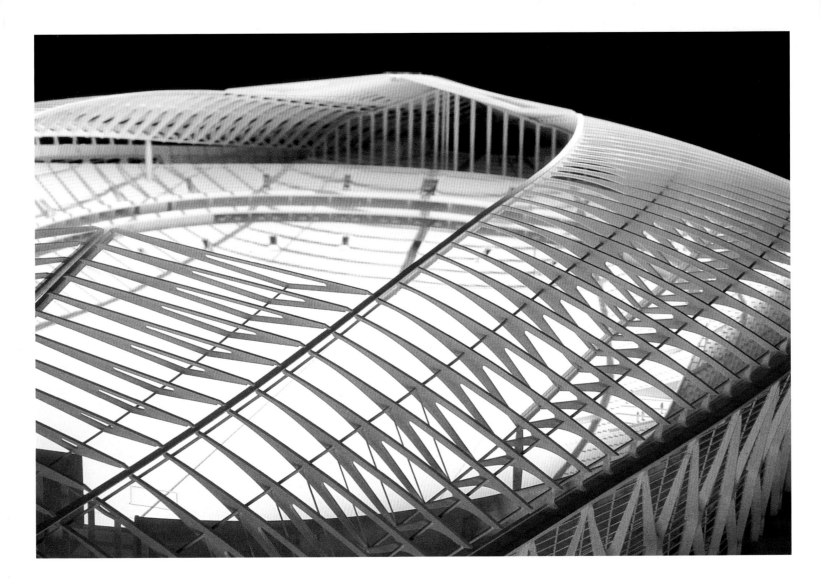

The goal of all these athletic facilities appears to be finding ways through the design to celebrate the idea of the *agon,* the gathering of the people who form a community, and honor the specific nature of the gathering, that is, to witness the human body performing various dynamic feats. Calatrava achieved this through the spatial arrangement of the athletic facility's site, in which the public space is always given emphasis. These ideas are also manifested through the configuration of the schemes which, in contrast to the formal and serene ambiance of the public spaces, appear much more vibrant and dynamic. Certainly the distribution of the weight in Calatrava's arch-holding-roof scheme, used extensively in these projects, is successful in its suggestion of the space's use for communal activities by implying the shape of a dome and resembling the body shifting from an upright position, as if in the act of pulling or supporting something.

Contrapposto is a very important motif that recurs frequently in Calatrava's work, and one can see this in most of his design objects, bridges, transportation terminals, and stadia. Contrapposto (Italian for "set against") was a method for depicting the body derived from ancient Greek art in which parts of the body are positioned in opposition to each other—as if suspended in time—to create a sense of movement. This method was canonized by the fifth-century-BCE Greek sculptor

and writer Polyclitos in his book *Kanon* and his masterful sculpture Doryphoros, which represented an athlete carrying a spear. When in contrapposto, the body appears to be at rest but is also dynamic, a stance commonly assumed by athletes before or after action, in which the majority of the body's weight rests on one leg that is pushed slightly backward. The other leg is bent at the knee and bears less weight. The chest, meanwhile, shifts slightly to one side of the body and the head counterbalances this by tilting the other way. In the statue of Nike, and in similar "windblown" sculptures from antiquity, drapery exaggerates the contrappostal stance and enhances the overall effect of movement. Marshaling his knowledge of mechanics, Calatrava has reinterpreted this idea and applied it to his architecture, which involves a sophisticated configuration of the structural members. He creates a zigzaging silhouette of the parts to maintain equilibrium, which in turn produces a varying profile that is occasionally streamlined to adapt to the weak areas that need strengthening. With these dynamic structures, he thoughtfully reflects and responds to the ambiance of activity and festivity and gives a unique identity to the place and the event.

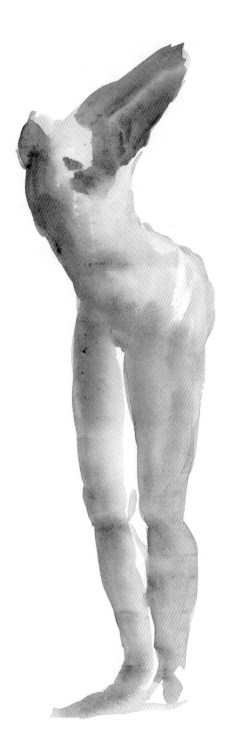

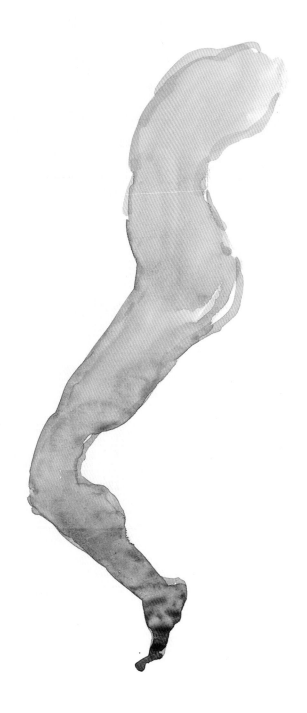

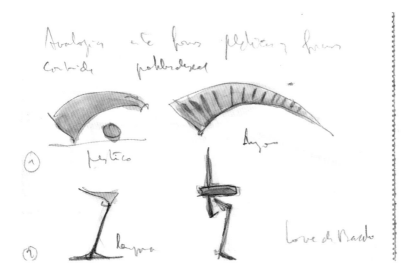

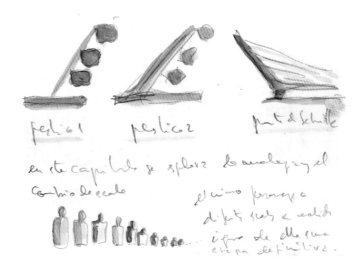

III

THE ATHENS OLYMPICS

After losing the centennial Summer Olympic Games in 1996 to Atlanta, Athens bid again in 1997 and was chosen to host the 2004 Olympic Games and Paralympics. The "return" of the modern games to Greece was an event of major historical, economic, and cultural significance and the news was received with great excitement around the world. However, there was also great anxiety because the existing facilities in Athens—a city with a population of 3 million—were far from adequate, and the city lacked experience with constructing such large-scale projects.

The event required creating infrastructure to accommodate the transportation needs of more than 10,000 athletes hailing from 200 countries, 20,000 journalists and press-related personnel, and an audience of hundreds of thousands of people from all over the world. Although a new airport and a very good metro system were already completed, the highway system and a 14-mile tram system were far from finished. In addition, Athens did not have enough swimming pools or an equestrian center; but more importantly, unlike most cities that had previously hosted the games, Athens needed to commission major permanent works of architecture.

Compounding the difficulties facing the city, very little construction was done until the last four years before the games. Rumors of catastrophic failures persisted throughout the construction of the various projects and continued until the last days leading up to the opening ceremonies. Adding to an already tense situation were fears of a terrorist attack. Greece mobilized its army, navy, and air force. NATO contributed security personnel, which turned the Athens Olympics into the most costly and security-conscious games in modern history.

PREVIOUS PAGE
**Olympic Stadium in Athens
at night**

BELOW
**Site plan of the Athens Olympic
Sports Complex**

OPPOSITE
**Model of the Athens Olympic
Sports Complex**

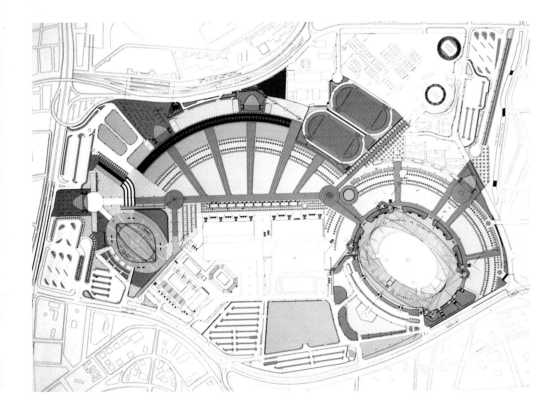

According to Susan Sachs of the *New York Times,* the Greek government estimated that in the last two weeks before the games "the bill for police training, bonuses, surveillance equipment and other security items [was] expected to come to at least $1.2 billion ... four times the amount paid for security by Sydney, Australia, the host of the 2000 Summer Games." Anticipatory anxiety reached a climax when, in the last days before the games with the entire city and the surrounding region still an immense workshop employing more than 4,000 Greek volunteers and many more Albanian and Pakistani immigrant workers preparing for the opening ceremonies, a zeppelinlike surveillance balloon appeared over the sky of Attica. Hired to watch over the capital, it was an ominous reminder of the zeppelin that hovered over Berlin during the 1936 Olympic Games.

On August 13, however, anxiety gave way to celebration when the Olympic torch reached the Olympic Stadium designed by Santiago Calatrava and the 2004 games officially began with an athlete's parade and a jubilant gala opening ceremony. On August 29, the games ended with the men's marathon in the white marble Panathinaiko Stadium in the heart of Athens, which was followed by another traditional Olympic parade in the stadium.

At the closing ceremony, Dr. Jacques Rogge, the president of the International Olympic Committee, officially announced, "These games were held in peace and brotherhood." The return of the Olympics to Athens was unanimously declared a success, and a major contribution to this success was Santiago Calatrava's architecture.

***

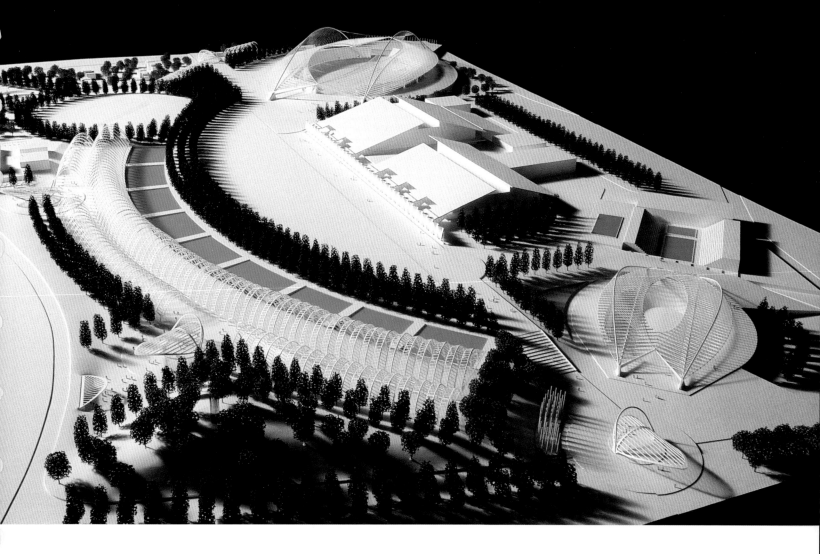

Following the decision by the International Olympic Committee to award Athens the 2004 games, the host city was obliged to improve and unify the existing Athens Olympic Sports Complex (OAKA) in Marousi, a northern suburb of Athens, and the surrounding area. The objective was to provide adequate facilities for the practical needs of the games, as well as a permanent center for future athletic and cultural events. The program contained the following list of requirements: to meet all the functional needs of the Olympic and Paralympic Games; to integrate all structures aesthetically and provide a common identity using both built and landscape elements; to accommodate the special needs of the visitors; and provide an efficient solution to waste management and other ecological concerns. The program also revealed a nationalistic agenda in its request for the use of local vegetation, including olive trees and cypresses.

The Athens Olympic Sports Complex was comprised of 199,000 square meters of plazas; 94,000 square meters of pedestrian pathways; 61,000 square meters of green areas; 29,000 square meters of water elements; 130,000 square meters of service facilities; and 178,000 square meters of parking and roads. In addition, the project required 2,500 new trees; 600 replanted trees; 160,000 shrubs; 8,500 fencing trees; and 400,000 cubic meters of landfill.

On October 9, 2001, Calatrava officially received the commission from city officials and the organizing committee to design the Athens Olympic Sports Complex and master plan—just three years before the games took place. As with the previous sports facilities discussed above, the major concern for his work for the games was the overall quality of the area within which his buildings were to be inserted. Given the poorly defined character of the setting in Marousi, organizing the site became a top priority.

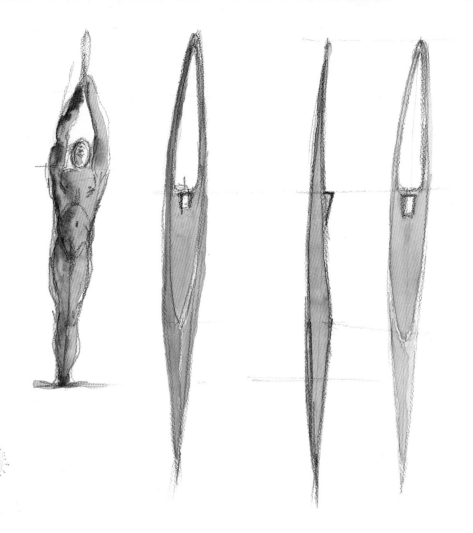

LEFT
**Drawing by Calatrava of the
torch for the Athens Olympics
from notebook 2002-602**

OPPOSITE
Torch for the Athens Olympics

FOLLOWING PAGES
**Aerial view of the Athens
Olympic Sports Complex**

With the commission in hand, Calatrava undertook the following projects, with the help of the project coordinator Leonidas Kikiras: reorganizing the existing 100-hectare area; a new roof for the Olympic Stadium; a new roof and refurbishing of the Velodrome; entrance plazas; and entrance canopies for the entire complex. In addition, on his own initiative he designed the Agora complex; a central Plaza of the Nations, which included tree-lined boulevards; a pair of arcade structures; his own version of an Olympic cauldron—a giant torch; a sculptural Nations Wall; a new warm-up area for athletes; pedestrian bridges and connections to public transportation; parking areas; bus terminals; and installations for all service elements. He also conceived of the idea for the Commons area to include circulation spines. The central circulation spine for the complex runs in an east-west direction, connecting the Olympic Stadium and the Velodrome. Perpendicular to this spine is a wide boulevard of trees that links the tennis courts, the new warm-up areas, and the Logistics Center.

OLYMPIC STADIUM ROOF

TOTAL HEIGHT

72 m

SURFACE COVERED BY ROOF

23,500 m²

LONGITUDINAL DISTANCE BETWEEN SUPPORTS

304 m

TRANSVERSAL LENGTH

206 m

TRANSVERSAL DISTANCE BETWEEN SUPPORTS

141 m

TOTAL WEIGHT OF THE STRUCTURE

18,000 tons

DIAMETER OF ARCH TUBE

3.25 m

DIAMETER OF TORSION TUBE

3.6 m

NUMBER OF CABLES

216 thin, 32 thick

The Olympic Stadium, used for the opening and closing ceremonies, track and field events, and men's soccer final, is covered with a roof of laminated glass. This glass is capable of reflecting up to 90 percent of the sunlight that hits it, a necessity for the sun-drenched region of Attica. The building itself is composed of a pair of bent "leaves." The Olympic flame was placed within the building at the structure's north end.

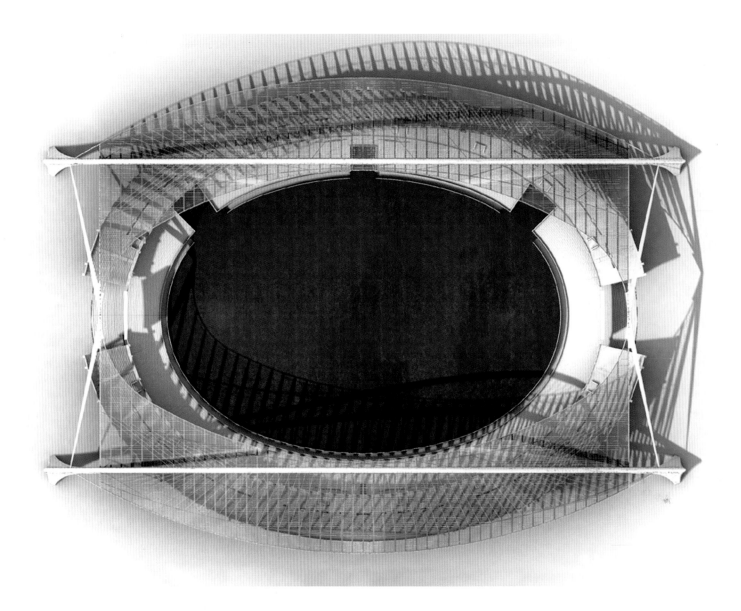

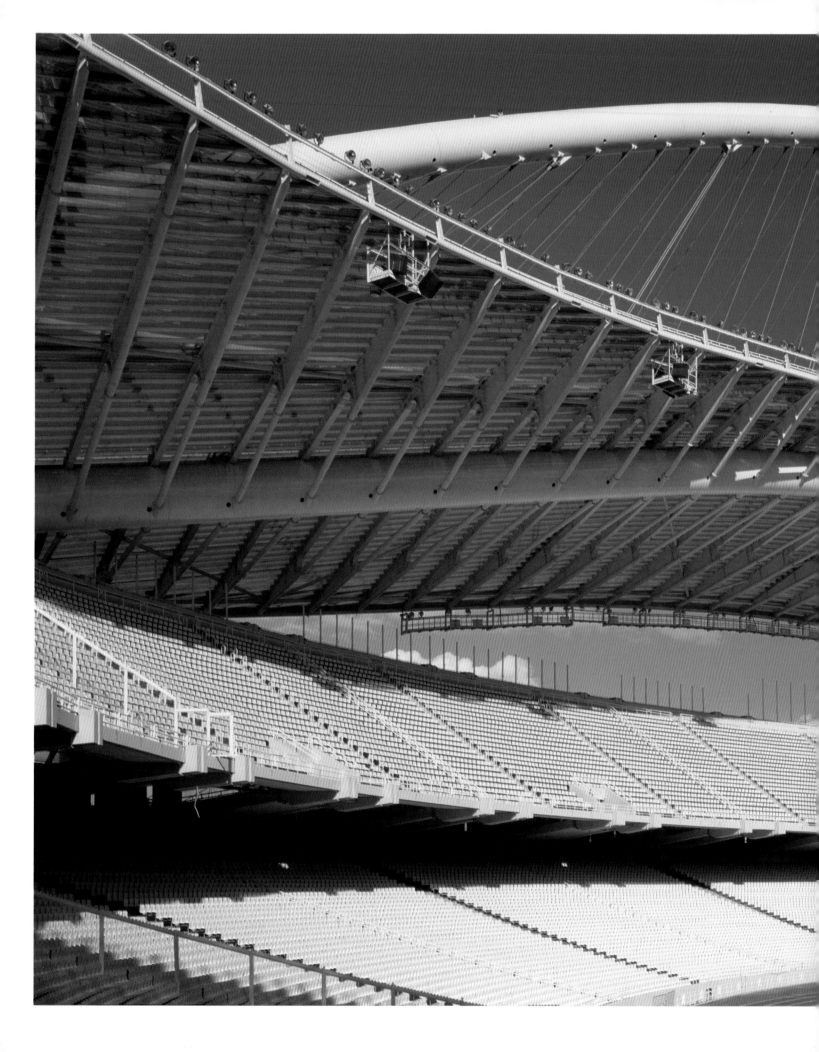

ABOVE AND OPPOSITE
**Structural details of Olympic
Stadium**

FOLLOWING PAGES
**View of suspended roof and
interior of stadium**

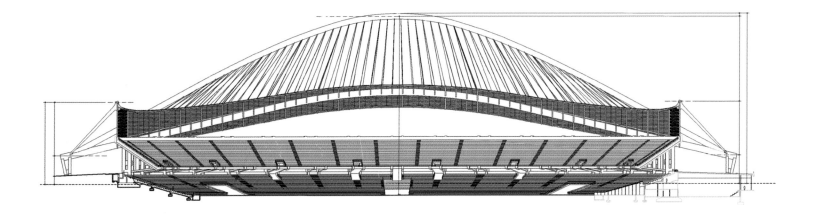

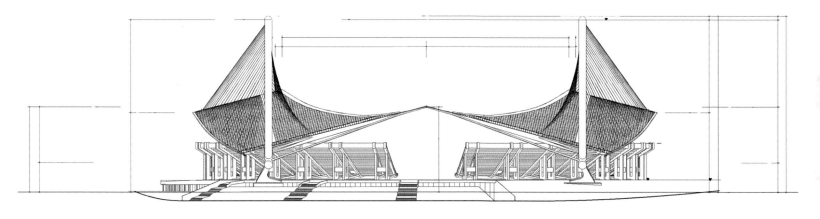

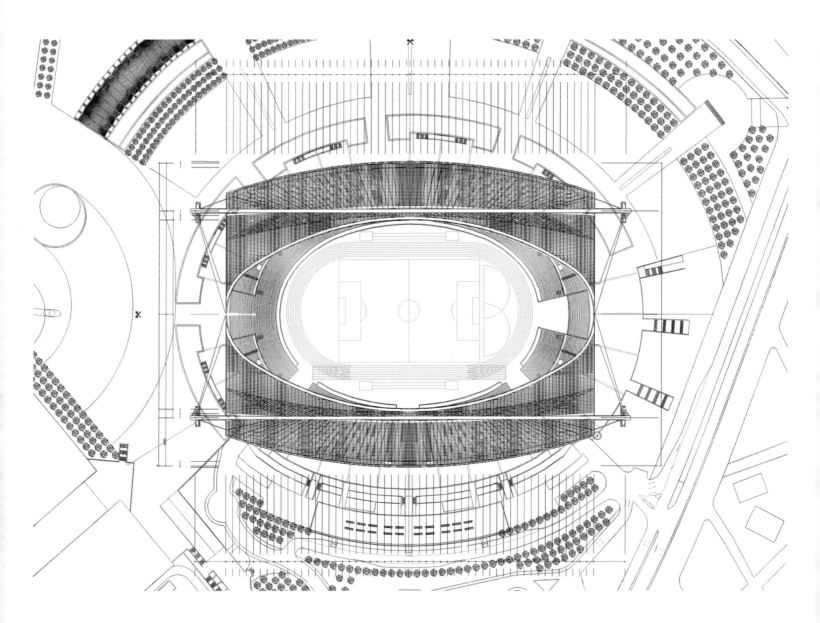

VELODROME ROOF

TOTAL HEIGHT

46 m

SURFACE COVERED BY ROOF

11,900 m²

LONGITUDINAL DISTANCE BETWEEN SUPPORTS

145 m

TRANSVERSAL LENGTH

109 m

TRANSVERSAL DISTANCE BETWEEN SUPPORTS

23 m

TOTAL WEIGHT OF THE STRUCTURE

4,000 tons

DIAMETER OF ARCH TUBE

1.3 m

DIAMETER OF TORSION TUBE

1.8 m

NUMBER OF CABLES

152

The Velodrome, used for indoor cycling events, is covered with a roof that is wood-clad on the interior (for better acoustics) and metal-clad on the exterior, with a central area of laminated glass that reflects sunlight. The bearing structure consists of a pair of bowstring-tied arches made of tubular steel.

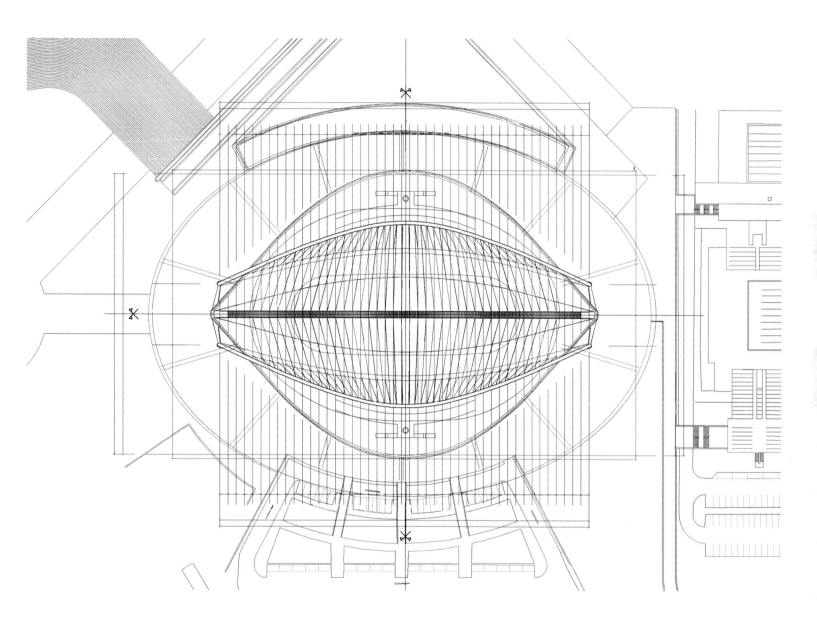

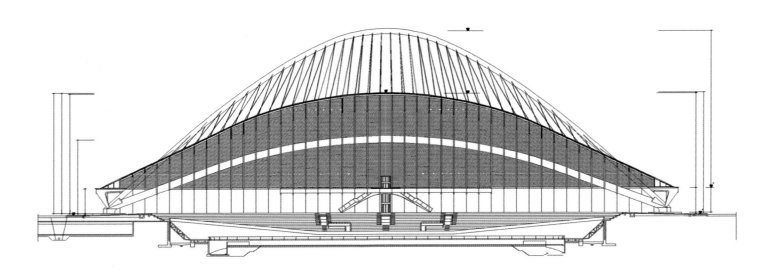

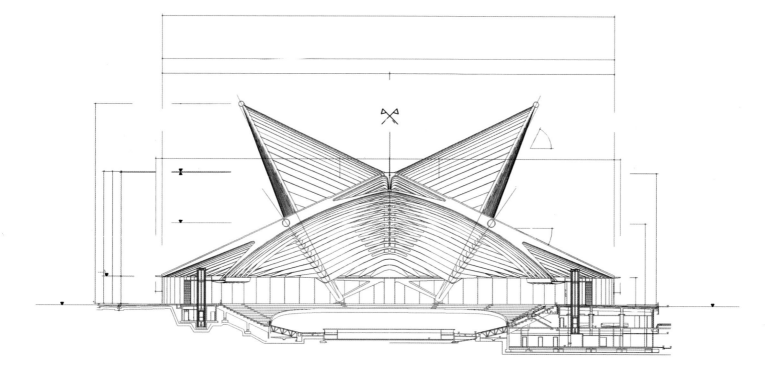

OPPOSITE AND ABOVE
Velodrome under construction

AGORA

NUMBER OF ARCHES
99

DISTANCE BETWEEN ARCHES
4.9 m

HEIGHT OF ARCHES
shortest 18.65 m
tallest 21.65 m

DISTANCE BETWEEN SUPPORTS
26 m

ANGLE OF THE STRUCTURE
A1: 66°
A2: 68.5°

LENGTH COVERED
480 m

WEIGHT OF THE STRUCTURE
1,300 tons

The Agora is comprised of two vaulted, open-air arcades that run along the northern edge of the site to create a shady, curving promenade. The tree-lined promenades alongside the Agora feature pools and fountains, offering visitors a bit of shade and cool air coming off the water. It leads around an artificial pond toward several of the competition areas. During the games, it was used as an entry point into the complex of Olympic buildings and sports venues. People congregated here on their way to and from the events. The structure has a special character in the evenings because it is adjacent to an arrangement of fountains and lights.

PREVIOUS PAGES
The Agora at dusk

FOLLOWING PAGES
The Agora at night

OPPOSITE
**View into the Agora with
Velodrome in the background**

ENTRANCE CANOPIES

WIDTH

54.5 m

LENGTH

44 m

HEIGHT

11 m

NUMBER OF GIRDERS

17

TOTAL WEIGHT

367 tons

Four entrance plazas provided ceremonial access
to the Athens Olympic Sports Complex. Two of
the plazas are located at opposite ends of a central
circulation spine, which runs between the Olympic
Stadium and the Velodrome. The other two, on the
north side of the complex, lead from the Irinis Elec-
tric Railway Station and the Neratziotissa pedestrian bridge to one of the two covered Agoras. Each
entrance gate is roofed with a vaulted steel canopy.

FOLLOWING PAGES
**Entrance canopy at
night with the Agora in
the foreground**

NATIONS WALL

TOTAL LENGTH

261 m

VERTICAL ELEMENTS

960

HEIGHT OF VERTICAL ELEMENTS

20 m

NUMBER OF MOTORS

480

MAXIMUM MOVEMENT OF THE
VERTICAL ELEMENTS

4 10°

LENGTH OF THE WAVE

12.5 m

NUMBER OF MAIN BEAMS

10 + 2 cantilevers of 5.5 m at the ends

NUMBER OF COLUMNS

11

DISTANCE BETWEEN COLUMNS

25 m

WEIGHT OF THE STRUCTURE

900 tons

The Plaza of the Nations occupies a sloping, semi-circular area at the heart of the complex, between the northern Agora and the central circulation spine. This area, which is reminiscent of a landscaped amphitheater, can accommodate as many as 300,000 people and can be used for shows and theatrical productions. It can also be used for screening events on the giant video display on the Nations Wall, a monumental tubular-steel wall sculpture. The wall is adjacent to the complex's Indoor Hall. Designed to move in a wavelike motion, the Nations Wall creates a play of light and shadow over the central circulation spine and Plaza of the Nations.

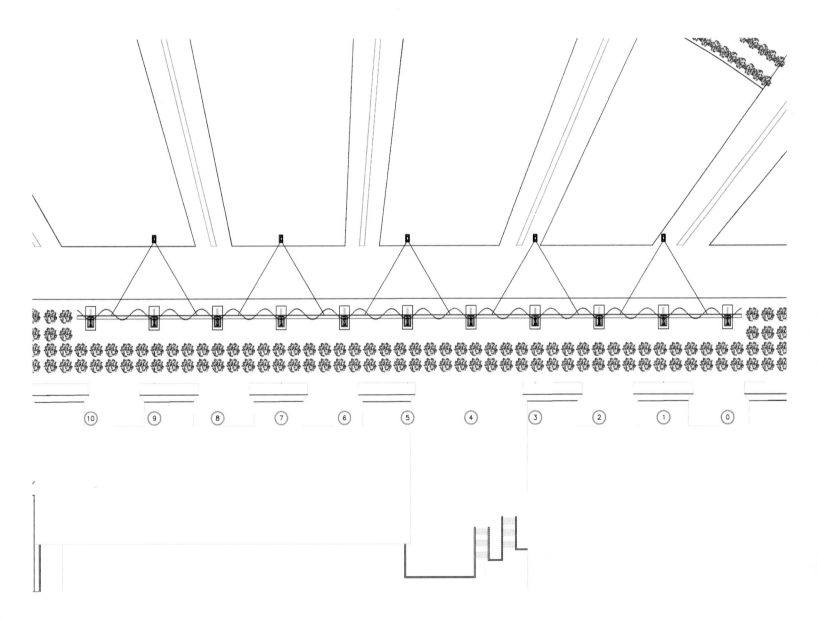

All the new structures by Calatrava were designed to allow, to the greatest extent possible, off-site fabrication, thereby reducing the need for on-site personnel and equipment and minimizing the interference with the other construction work on the existing buildings. Work done on site, especially the assemblage of the enormous roof, was not easy, but it was completed with aplomb and on time.

As with the other athletic facilities that Calatrava has designed in the past, the structures of the Olympic Games in Athens are clearly set apart from the delicate landscape that surrounds them. Yet they do not scar the soft, smooth slopes of the neighboring mountains and do not disturb or erase the historical import of the area. With his use of the soaring arch motif, combined with the occasional contrappostal element, Calatrava gave definition—both aesthetic and symbolic—to a

group of disparate buildings on a poorly planned site and created a cohesive, and more importantly, inspiring Olympic complex. And, remarkably, he achieved this while making reference and paying homage to the historical legacy of the site and the games without reverting to the use of anachronistic classical motifs.

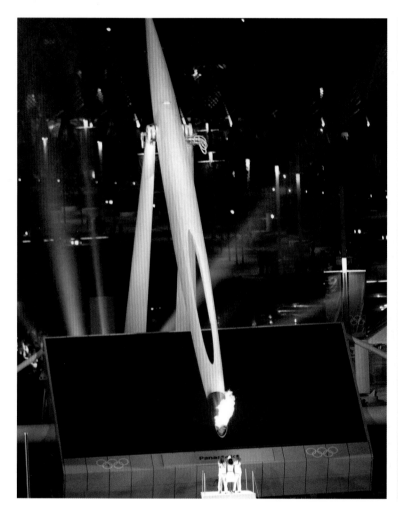

IV

CALATRAVA'S GAMES

In his dissertation, Calatrava presented the principals, operations, and analytical steps through which one can generate a systematic repertory of folding structural frames. As discussed in Chapter II, the pragmatic goal of his study was the development of a geometrical-mechanical system made out of bars and joints that could create all possible folding polyhedral frame structures that could be used as roofs, canopies, or doors by being expanded, contracted, opened, and closed by means of a mechanical device. Calatrava intended for the system to function as a toolbox enabling designers to conceive buildings unbounded by the constraints of static space and to explore the possibilities of an infinite variety of moving structures, like the Nations Wall created for the Athens Olympics.

And because the system acted like a sophisticated compass, it could generate a very large number of possible complex curved surfaces. Some of the surfaces proposed by this system were realized in the intricate configurations of Calatrava's Agora, among many other projects in his body of work.

OPPOSITE

Detail of the Agora arch

Whether it was used to represent folding surfaces or to describe curved surfaces, it was critical to develop a system of frame structures that could move without its elements interfering with each other. This obliged Calatrava to employ branches of mathematics and mechanical engineering to

model geometrical transformations of three-dimensional frames and articulate the mechanical connectors in the joints. Given his skill at analysis and his ability to conceive form by means of a rigorous system that he developed, it is interesting that Calatrava created, simultaneous to this research, countless series of notebooks containing freehand sketches not only of structures but also a variety of bodies, both human and animal.

Throughout these sketchbooks, the human figure is represented in many different positions, as if he was documenting the body engaged in different sports. In their arrangement on the page and serial quality, they are also very reminiscent of ancient Greek friezes.

Drawings by Calatrava from
notebooks:
2000-1215-27 [BELOW, LEFT];
2000-1215-19 [BELOW, RIGHT];
2000-1215-09 [BOTTOM, LEFT];
2000-1215-18 [BOTTOM, RIGHT]

BELOW
Drawing by Calatrava from
notebook 2001-1101-04

OPPOSITE, TOP
Drawing by Calatrava from
notebook 2002-100-21

OPPOSITE, BOTTOM
Drawing by Calatrava from
notebook 2002-10022

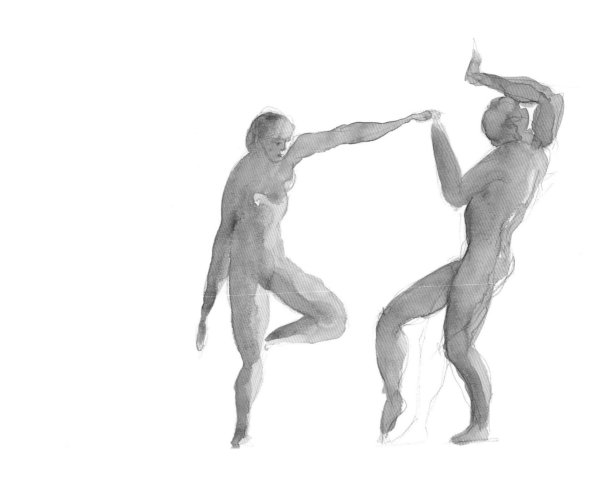

Why would a designer so capable of rigorous, systematic thinking, whose scientific research was so productive, invest time in the seemingly unscientific, unrigorous endeavor of drawing various types of structures, their details, and the human body? Are the sketches that fill those notebooks simply doodles, an escape from designing real structures or are they another kind of research informing his architecture? And if the latter is true, how do the drawings benefit his work?

Calatrava's dissertation theorizes that all possible folding polyhedra could be generated from the system he developed, that is, the system could breed *analytically,* bit by bit and exhaustively all options for any given design problem. In reality, however, generating such a comprehensive repertory of schemes would be nearly impossible. These schemes would then have to be examined, tested, evaluated, and rejected or chosen based on their suitability to real-world constraints. It is a process that would demand resources of time, memory, and energy not available to humans or machines. This process of analysis, while ingenious, is limited. To generate a solution to a design problem another mode of thinking must be employed, one that is

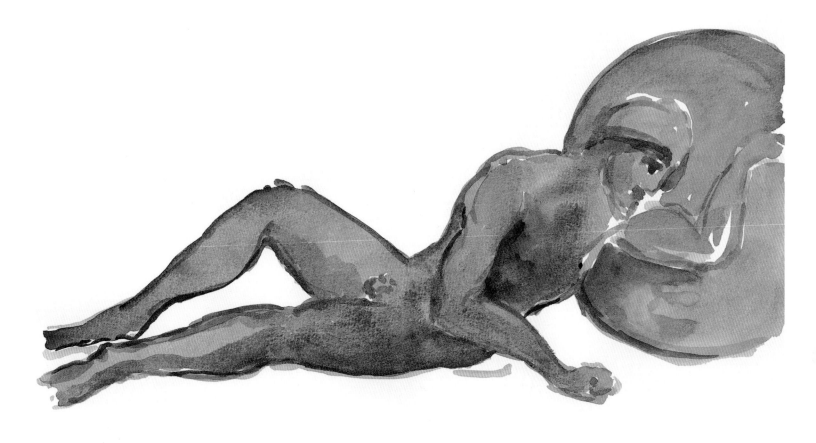

diametrically opposed but complementary to analysis, a "quick and dirty" heuristics—analogy. As opposed to the gradual, "hill-climbing" approximation used to achieve an optimal scheme that is analysis, design analogy is saltational. It allows the designer to jump to possible design schemes by recruiting them associatively from available precedents, artifacts, or natural creatures that serve as paradigms. Accordingly, designers working in this mode do not search or make computations—they are inspired. And, as the etymology of "inspire" suggests, conceiving the optimal schemes is like breathing: effortless, spontaneous, and devoid of formal research. Calatrava is the unique designer who engages both analysis and analogy in his work.

The answer to the question posed above—why Calatrava spends so much of his time making sketches—is analogy. The sketches present possible solutions through their exploration and transformation of existing precedents by moving their members to approximate the structural constraints of the design problem. In this way, the invention of

OPPOSITE
**Drawing by Calatrava from
notebook 2003-116-11**

RIGHT
**Drawing by Calatrava from
notebook 2003-116-14**

a new form, an unknown, complex shape of a folding structure to cover an intricate opening, or a
new, curved configuration of a bridging structure
is aided by recruiting from the repertory of precedents from nature or the body. Thus, the collec-
tion of Calatrava's sketches—which includes racing
bulls, plants, flying birds, and a cornucopia of
combinations of the members of the human body
engaged in running, jumping, bending, leaning,
carrying, holding, pulling, and supporting—forms
a kind of thesaurus that offers a true design tool.

Yet, beyond their use in pursuit of an end—a design
solution—just as the gathering of the athletes
and their actions in the stadium, so Calatrava's
arrangements of the human figure in these sketchbooks offer a special cognitive pleasure—to borrow

Heracletus's brilliant aphorism about the oracle
in Delphi: they neither inform nor conceal but
indicate the search for *teliotis.* In other words,
Calatrava's drawings make us look at the world
with different eyes without being didactic, and
they arouse our desire for its possession without
making it seem unapproachable. The drawings
are Calatrava's *agon,* Calatrava's games.

SANTIAGO CALATRAVA: THE ATHENS OLYMPICS

**Drawings by Calatrava from
notebook 2003-1111**

TOP

Drawings by Calatrava from
notebook 2002-1218

ABOVE

Drawings by Calatrava from
notebook 2003-120

FROM TOP TO BOTTOM
Drawings by Calatrava
from notebooks 2002-1217,
2002-1209, 2002-1210, and
2002-1211

BIBLIOGRAPHY

MONOGRAPHS

Blaser, W. *Santiago Calatrava: Ingenieur Architektur.* Basel, Switzerland: Birkhäuser Verlag, 1989.

Calatrava, S. *Alpine Bridges.* Weinfeld: Wolfau-Druck AG Christof Mühlemann, 2004.

Frampton, K., A.C. Webster, and A. Tischhauser. *Calatrava Bridges.* Zurich: Birkhäuser Verlag, 2002.

Harbison, R. *Creatures from the Mind of the Engineer, The Architecture of Santiago Calatrava.* Zurich: Artemis Verlag, 1992.

Jodidio, Ph. *Oriente Station.* Lisbon: Centralivros Lda., 1998.

———. *Santiago Calatrava.* Cologne: Taschen , 1998.

Kausel, C.L., and A. Pendleton-Jullian, eds. *Santiago Calatrava—Conversations with Students.* New York: Princeton Architectural Press, 2002.

Klein, B. *Santiago Calatrava: Bahnhof Stadelhofen, Zürich.* Tübingen and Berlin: Ernst Wasmuth Verlag, 1993.

Lefaivre, L. *Santiago Calatrava Creative Process II: Sketchbooks.* Basel, Switzerland: Birkhäuser Verlag, 2001.

Levin, M. *Calatrava, drawings and sculptures.* Weinfeld: Wolfau-Druck Rudolf Mühlemann, 2000.

———. *Santiago Calatrava Artworks.* Basel, Switzerland: Birkhäuser Verlag, 2003.

Schulze, F. *Building a Masterpiece: Milwaukee Art Museum.* Manchester, Vermont: Hudson Hills Press, 2001.

Sharp, D., ed. *Santiago Calatrava.* London: Art/E&FN Spon, 1992.

Tischauser, A., and S. von Moos. *Public Buildings.* Basel, Switzerland: Birkhäuser Verlag, 1998.

Tzonis, A. *Santiago Calatrava: The Complete Works.* New York: Rizzoli International Publications, 2004.

———. *Santiago Calatrava Creative Process I: Fundamentals.* Basel, Switzerland: Birkhäuser Verlag, 2001.

———. *Santiago Calatrava: The Poetics of Movement.* New York: Universe Publishing, 1999.

Tzonis, A., and R. Caso Donadei. *Santiago Calatrava: The Bridges.* New York: Universe Publishing, 2005.

Tzonis. A., and L. Lefaivre. *Movement, Structure and the Work of Santiago Calatrava.* Basel, Switzerland: Birkhäuser Verlag, 1994.

Webster, A.C., and K. Frampton. *Santiago Calatrava.* Zurich: Schriftenreihe 15, Schule und Museum fur Gestaltung, 1992.

**EXHIBITION PUBLICATIONS, SPECIAL ISSUES OF
PERIODICALS, PROJECT MONOGRAPHS**

"Santiago Calatrava 1983–1989." *El Croquis* 38, 1989.

"Santiago Calatrava 1990–1992." *El Croquis* 57, 1992.

"Santiago Calatrava 1983–1993." Valencia, Spain:
   La Lontja, 1993. Reprinted as an editorial in *El Croquis*.

Cullen, M.S., and M. Kieren. *Calatrava Berlin Five Projects /
   Fünf projekte*. Basel, Switzerland: Birkhäuser Verlag, 1994.

Fernández Galiano, L. "Santiago Calatrava 1983–1996."
   AV Monografías 61, 1996.

Hashimshoni, R. *Santiago Calatrava, Structures and
   Movement*. Haifa, Israel: Technion, 1997.

Hauser, H. *Kontroverse Beitrage zu einem unstrittenen
   Bautypus*. Stuttgart: n.p., 1993.

Lefaivre, L. *Santiago Calatrava, Wie ein Vogel / Like a Bird*.
   Geneva and Milan: Skira, 2003.

McQuaid, M. *Santiago Calatrava, Structure and Expression*.
   New York: Museum of Modern Art, 1992.

Molinari, L. *Santiago Calatrava*. Milan: Skira, 1998.

Polano, S. *Santiago Calatrava, Complete Works*. Milan:
   Electa, 1996.

Tischauser, A., and T. Kobler. *Santiago Calatrava:
   Dynamische Gleichgewichte Neue Projekte / Dynamic
   Equilibrium Recent Projects*. Zurich: Artemis Verlag, 1991.

Webster, A.C., and K. Frampton. "Santiago Calatrava."
   Museum für Gestaltung, Zurich; Wolfau-Druck Rudolf
   Mühlemann, Weinfeld, 1992.

BIOGRAPHY

1951
Santiago Calatrava Valls born in Valencia, Spain

1968
School graduation in Valencia

1968–69
Attends Valencia School of Arts and Crafts

1969–74
Studies architecture at the Escuela Técnica Superior de Arquitectura de Valencia, qualifying as an architect, followed by a postgraduate course in urbanism

1975–79
Studies civil engineering at the Swiss Federal Institute of Technology (ETH), Zurich

1979–81
Doctorate in Technical Science at ETH; Ph.D. dissertation: *On the Foldability of Space Frames*

Assistant at the Institute for Building Statics and Construction and Aerodynamics and Lightweight Construction at the ETH

1981
Architectural and engineering practice established in Zurich

1982
Membership, International Association for Bridge & Structural Engineering, Zurich

1985
9 Sculptures by Santiago Calatrava, exhibition, Jamileh Weber Gallery, Zurich

1987
Member of the BSA (Union of Swiss Architects)

Auguste Perret UIA Prize (Union Internationale d'Architectes), Brighton

Member of the International Academy of Architecture, Sofia, Bulgaria

Participation at the 17th Triennale, Milan

Santiago Calatrava, exhibition, Museum of Architecture, Basel, Switzerland

1988
City of Barcelona Art Prize for the Bach de Roda Bridge, Barcelona

Premio de la Asociación de la Prensa (Press Association Award), Valencia

IABSE Prize, International Association of Bridge and Structural Engineering, Helsinki, Finland

FAD Prize, Fomento de las Artes y del Diseño, Spain

Fritz Schumacher Prize for Urbanism, Architecture and Engineering, Hamburg, Germany

Fazlur Rahman Khan International Fellowship for Architecture and Engineering

1989
Second architectural and engineering practice established in Paris

Honorary Member of the BDA (Bund Deutscher Architekten)

Santiago Calatrava, traveling exhibition, New York, St. Louis, Chicago, Los Angeles, Toronto, and Montreal

1990

Médaille d'Argent de la Recherche et de la Technique, Fondation Académie d'Architecture 1970, Paris

1991

European Glulam Award (Glued Laminated Timber Construction), Munich, Germany

Santiago Calatrava, exhibition, Suomen Rakennustaiteen Museum, Helsinki

City of Zurich Award for Good Building 1991, for Stadelhofen Railway Station, Zurich

Retrospective—Dynamic Equilibrium, exhibition, Museum of Design, Zurich

1992

CEOE Foundation, VI Dragados y Construcciones Prize for Alamillo Bridge

Honorary Member of Real Academia de Bellas Artes de San Carlos, Valencia

Member of the Europe Academy, Cologne

Retrospective, exhibition, Dutch Institute for Architecture, Rotterdam, The Netherlands

Gold Medal, Institute of Structural Engineers, London

Brunel Award, for Stadelhofen Railway Station, Zurich

Santiago Calatrava—Retrospective, exhibition, Royal Institute of British Architects, London

Retrospective, exhibition, Arkitektur Museet, Stockholm

1993

II Honor Prize, from the City of Pedreguer for Urban Arquitectonic Merit, Pedreguer, Spain

Santiago Calatrava—Bridges, exhibition, Deutsches Museum, Munich

Structure and Expression, exhibition, Museum of Modern Art, New York

Honorary Member of the Royal Institute of British Architects, London

Santiago Calatrava, exhibition, La Lontja Museum, Valencia

Santiago Calatrava, exhibition, Overbeck Society Pavilion, Lübeck, Germany

Santiago Calatrava, exhibition, Architecture Centre, Gammel Dok, Copenhagen

Doctor Honoris Causa, Polytechnic University of Valencia

Medalla de Honor al Fomento de la Invención, Fundación Garcia Cabrerizo, Madrid

City of Toronto Urban Design Award, for the BCE Place Galeria, Toronto

World Economic Forum Davos honors Santiago Calatrava as Global Leader for Tomorrow

1994

Santiago Calatrava—Recent Projects, exhibition, Bruton Street
   Gallery, London

Doctor Honoris Causa, University of Seville

Santiago Calatrava—Buildings and Bridges, exhibition,
   Museum of Applied and Folk Arts, Moscow

Creu de Sant Jordi, Generalitat de Catalunya, Barcelona

Doctor Honoris Causa of Letters in Environmental Studies,
   Herriot-Watt University, Edinburgh

Santiago Calatrava—The Dynamics of Equilibrium, exhibition,
   Gallery MA, Tokyo

Santiago Calatrava, exhibition, Arqueria de los Nuevos
   Ministerios, Madrid

Santiago Calatrava, exhibition, Sala de Arte "La Recova,"
   Santa Cruz de Tenerife, Spain

Fellow Honoris Causa, The Royal Incorporation of
   Architects, Scotland

Honorary Member of Colegio de Arquitectos, Mexico City

Maître D'Oeuvre, Grande halle de la gare TGV Lyon-
   Saint-Exupéry Airport, Rhône, France

1995

Santiago Calatrava, exhibition, Centro Cultural de Belem,
   Lisbon

Santiago Calatrava—Construction and Movement, exhibition,
   Fondazione Angelo Masieri, Venice

Doctor Honoris Causa of Science, University College, Salford

Santiago Calatrava, exhibition, Navarra Museum, Pamplona

Award for Good Building 1983–1993, Canton of Lucerne,
   for the railway station and square

Certificate for the Practice of Professional Engineering,
   Frosinone

1996

Medalla de Oro al Mérito de las Bellas Artes, Ministry
   of Culture, Granada

Santiago Calatrava, exhibition, Archivo Foral, Bilbao

*Santiago Calatrava, Bewegliche Architekturen—bündel
   fächer welle,* exhibition, Museum of Design, Zurich

Santiago Calatrava—opere e progetti 1980–1996, exhibition,
   Palazzo della Ragione, Padua

Mostra Internazionale di Scultura All'aperto, exhibition, Vira
   Gambarogno, Ascona and Bellinzona, Italy

Doctor Honoris Causa of Science, University of Strathclyde,
   Glasgow

Santiago Calatrava—Quarto Ponte sul Canal Grande, exhibition,
   Spazio Olivetti, Venice

Santiago Calatrava—Sculpture, exhibition, Government
   Building, St. Gallen, Switzerland

Santiago Calatrava—Kunst ist Bau—Bau ist Kunst, exhibition,
   Department of Building, Basel

Santiago Calatrava, exhibition, Milwaukee Art Museum,
   Milwaukee, Wisconsin

Santiago Calatrava—City Point, A New Tower for the City,
   exhibition, Britannic Tower, London

1997

Doctor of Science Honoris Causa, University of Technology, Delft

Santiago Calatrava—Structures and Movement, exhibition, National Museum of Science, Haifa, Israel

European Award for Steel Structures, reconstruction of the Kronprinzenbrücke, Berlin

Louis Vuitton–Moët Hennessy Art Prize, Paris

Master de Oro del Forum de Alta Dirección, Madrid

Doctor Honoris Causa of Engineering, Milwaukee School of Engineering, Milwaukee, Wisconsin

Structural Engineer License by the State of Illinois Department of Professional Engineering, License No. 081-005441, granted November (Renewed in 1998 and 2000)

Temporary License for the Practice of Professional Engineering by the State of California Board of Professional Engineers and Land Surveyors (Renewed in 1998)

1998

Member of Les Arts et Lettres, Paris

Santiago Calatrava—Work in Progress, exhibition, Triennale, Milan

Brunel Award, Madrid—Oriente Station, Lisbon Multimodal Station, Lisbon

Lecture series for the School of Architecture and Design at Massachusetts Institute of Technology, Cambridge

Lecture series, winter semester, Architecture Department, ETH, Zurich

1999

Doctor Honoris Causa of Civil Engineering, Università degli Studi di Cassino

Principe de Asturias, Art Prize, Spain

Doctor Honoris Causa of Technology, University of Lund, Lund, Sweden

Foreign Member of the Royal Swedish Academy of Engineering Sciences, IVA

License for the Practice of Professional Engineering by the State of Texas, Board of Professional Engineers, License No. 85263

Grau Grande Oficial da Ordem do Mérito, Chancelaria das Ordens Honorificas Portuguesas, Lisbon

Gold Medal, The Concrete Society, London

Honorable Mention for Canadian Consulting Engineering Awards for the Mimico Creek Bridge, Toronto

2000

Santiago Calatrava, traveling exhibition, Montevideo, Uruguay and Buenos Aires, Argentina

Doctor Honoris Causa of Architecture, Universita degli Studi di Ferrara

Honorary Fellowship, Royal Architectural Institute of Canada College of Fellows

"Das Goldene Dach 2000" (The Golden Roof), Structural Completion of the Pfalzkeller, St. Gallen

Fellowship, Institute for Urban Design, New York

Honorary Fellowship, National Academy of Architecture, Monterrey, Mexico

Lecture Series for the School of Architecture and Design at Massachusetts Institute of Technology, Cambridge

Guest of Honor, Mexico City

Santiago Calatrava Scultore, Ingegnere, Architetto, exhibition, Palazzo Strozzi, Florence

Beauty and Efficiency, a Challenge of Modern Infrastructure, The IVA Royal Technology Forum, Stockholm

2000 Algur H. Meadows Award for Excellence in the Arts, Meadows School of Arts, Dallas

Temporary License and Certificate of Practice for Engineering, OAA Ontario Association of Architects

Gold Medal, Círculo de Bellas Artes, Valencia

Honorary Academician, Real Academia de Bellas Artes de San Fernando, Madrid

2001

Prize Exitos 2000 to the best architectural work, for the Science Museum in Valencia, Madrid

Calatrava: Architect, Sculptor, Engineer, exhibition, National Gallery Alexandros Soutzos Museum, Athens

Calatrava: Poetics of Movement, exhibition, Meadows Museum, Southern Methodist University, Dallas

Award for Excellence in Design for the Time Capsule, American Museum of Natural History, New York

Temporary License for the Practice of Professional Engineering by the State of Wisconsin Board of Architects, Landscape Architects, Professional Engineers, Designers and Land Surveyors

Santiago Calatrava Esculturas y Dibujos, exhibition, IVAM Centre Julio González, Valencia

Calatrava xx/iix, exhibition, Form and Design Center, Malmö, Sweden

European Award for Steel Structures for the Europe Bridge over the Loire River, Orléans, France

Calatrava, exhibition, Teloglion Foundation, Thessaloniki, Greece

2002

Best of 2001 prize for the design of the Milwaukee Art Museum Extension, *Time,* New York

"Il Principe e L'Architetto" prize for the design of the Quarto Ponte sul Canal Grande in Venice, Architettura e Design per la Cittá, Bologna

The Sir Misha Black Medal, Royal College of Art, London

Prize 2002 The Best Large Structural Project for the Milwaukee Art Museum Addition, The Structural Engineers Association of Illinois

Santiago Calatrava, traveling exhibition, Palacio de Minería, Mexico City and Museo de Arte Moderno, Santo Domingo, Dominican Republic

The Leonardo da Vinci Medal for an outstanding contribution to international engineering education, SEFIRENZE 2000, Florence

2003

Medalla al Mérito a las Bellas Artes, Real Academia de
San Carlos de Valencia, Valencia

Like a Bird, exhibition, Kunsthistorisches Museum,
Vienna, Austria

Grande Médaille d'Or, Architecture, Académie
D'Architecture, Paris

The European Steel Design Award for the Roof of the
University of Zurich

The Silver Beam Award of the Swedish Institute of Steel
Construction, Gothenburg, Sweden

The Illuminating Design Award of Merit of the Illuminating
Engineering Society of North America, New York

2004

WTC Project, exhibition, Museum of Modern Art, New York

Golden Plate Award, Academy of Achievement, Chicago

Doctor Scientiarium Honoris Causa, Technion Israel
Institute of Technology, Haifa

Tall Buildings, exhibition, Museum of Modern Art, New York

The Architect's Studio, exhibition, Henry Art Gallery, Seattle,
Washington

Outstanding Structure Award to The Milwaukee Art
Museum Addition, The International Association for
Bridge and Structural Engineering, Milwaukee, Wisconsin

Outstanding Project Award to the Milwaukee Art
Museum Addition, National Council of Structural
Engineers Associations, Milwaukee, Wisconsin

Gestalten und Konstruieren in Personalunion, 10th Holcim
Concrete Symposium 2004, Zurich

Gold Medal, Queen Sofia Spanish Institute, New York

2005

AIA Gold Medal, American Institute of Architects,
Washington, D.C.

Eugene McDermott Award in the Arts by the Council
for the Arts at Massachusetts Institute of Technology,
Cambridge

2005 MIPIN Awards for Turning Torso as best residential
building in the category "Residential Developments"

ATHENS OLYMPIC SPORTS COMPLEX CREDITS

The following individuals were instrumental in the
realization of the Olympic Complex:

Athanasios Sklavenitis

Ioannis Ventourakis

Dimitris Kirimlidis